Schooling Options

Choosing the Best for You & Your Child

Elaine K. McEwan

Harold Shaw Publishers
Wheaton, Illinois

To Richard,
my friend, mentor, and husband

ISBN 0-87788-753-5

Cover photo © Jim Whitmer

Library of Congress Cataloging-in-Publication Data

McEwan, Elaine K., 1941-
   Schooling options : choosing the best for you & your child / Elaine McEwan.
      p.   cm.
   Includes bibliographical references (p.).
   ISBN 0-87788-753-5
   1. School, Choice of. 2. Education—Parent participation. 3. Education—Aims and objectives.
   I. Title.
LB1027.9.M39   1991
370.11—dc20   90-49568
                                   CIP

---

99 98 97 96 95 94 93 92 91

10 9 8 7 6 5 4 3 2 1

Contents

Off to School

When my first child went off to kindergarten, I experienced all of the usual emotions. Not only was she leaving the nest, but in those new surroundings she would be instructed, examined, and evaluated. Would she measure up? Would she have fun? Would she like school? Would she learn?

More important, *what* would she learn? Would she learn what her father and I as Christians believed to be worthwhile and true?

As Christian parents, what did we expect from our child's schooling experience? What did we want her to be like when she completed her formal education?

Our academic goals were similar to those articulated by educational historian Diane Ravitch: "to read and write fluently in both English and a foreign language; to speak articulately; to listen carefully; to learn to participate in the give-and-take of group discussion; to learn self-discipline and to develop the capacity for deferred gratification; to read and appreciate good literature; to have a strong knowledge of history, both of our own nation and of others; to appreciate the values of a free, democratic society; to understand science, mathematics, technology, and the natural world; to become engaged in the arts, both as a participant and as one capable of appreciating aesthetic excellence."[1]

But in addition to those academic goals, we also had spiritual, social, and emotional goals. Among those that we believed to be important were strong self-esteem, the ability to articulate and defend the Christian faith, academic and personal honesty, a questioning mind, and the ability to have and be a friend.

The choice of where your child will go to school—public, Christian, or home—is one of the most important choices you will make as parent. For some families, the choice has to be reconsidered every fall as their children move through their schooling years. But as I look back on that day my first child left for school, I see clearly that all the effort we invested in making that decision has proved to be more than worthwhile.

Today, Christian parents trying to choose the best education for their children are faced with bewildering opportunities—and sometimes frightening hazards. Each option presents advantages. Yet the costs to you— in terms of money, time, risk, personal commitment, and peace of mind—make the decision a complicated one.

To add to the tangle, the views of many Christians seem set in concrete. They're convinced that their choice is the only one that a concerned believer could *possibly* agree with. As you approach your schooling choice, you should resign yourself to the fact that whatever you decide will make someone you know doubt your convictions.

While you may not be able to verbalize all of the goals you have for your child, you need to know that the educational choice you make will have a sizeable impact on what your child will become at the age of eighteen. There are dozens of books on the market that make a case for one schooling option over another. This book will not do that. There are dozens of authors who set forth persuasive arguments for their particular point of view. This author will not do that. What I *will* do is present you with a six-step process that can help clarify the issues for you, and give you confidence to make the best schooling choice for *your* child.

1

In the Beginning . . .

*E*ach year I consult with dozens of parents who are trying to make an important decision—where to send their children to school. The community where we live offers many options. Perhaps that is why their decision is such a difficult one. The political environment is supportive of the home-schooling movement and there are numerous support groups for home schoolers. Dozens of parents home-school their children. There are several excellent Christian schools, both church-affiliated and independent. They have strong academic records and outstanding reputations. There are at least two alternative schools, one for gifted students and another espousing the Montessori philosophy. And finally, the public school system is very well regarded. There are Christian teachers, administrators, and school board members actively involved in governance, policy making, and teaching in our public schools.

Some parents know exactly what they want before they come to my office. They are only looking for someone to confirm that they have made the right decision. But many are genuinely confused. They don't know how to make their way through the claims and counterclaims.

I recently appeared on a radio talk show with a home-school advocate, a Christian school headmaster, and a public school administrator. As the author of an article on schooling options, I was the "neutral" member of the panel. The discussion became heated as panel members attempted to defend their "positions." Participants from the radio audience were equally animated as they called in their "success" and "horror" stories from all perspectives. As I drove home, I reflected on the evening and drew three conclusions. First, parents, especially Christians, care more deeply about the schooling of their children than almost any other issue in their lives. Secondly, individuals—both educators and parents—frequently become embroiled in the "rightness" or "wrongness" of the choices and fail to look at what is best for the child. And, thirdly, Christian educators, no matter where they do their "educating," do everyone a disservice when they fail to recognize that we share a collective responsibility for the education of all of the children in our country.

Those conclusions have led me to four assumptions upon which this book will be based. First, I am assuming that *as a parent you believe that how your children will be schooled is one of your most important responsibilities.* The Scriptures confirm that. They tell us to "train a child in the way he should go, and when he is old he will not turn from it" (Proverbs 22:6). We commonly view this exhortation as a reference to Christian training only, but I believe the words encompass all areas of human development—intellectual, emotional, social, and physical, as well as spiritual. Each area must be addressed by the Christian parent who wants to obey God's Word. I am assuming that you will give the choice of your child's schooling option at least as much consideration as you give the purchase of a new home or automobile.

The second assumption is that *whatever schooling choice you make, you have a biblical commandment to do your part at home.* A child's education begins long before he goes to school, and the potential for learning in the preschool years is enormous. Nor does informal learning cease the minute a child begins his formal schooling. We cannot totally delegate the responsibility for education to someone else, or pay them to do what we are charged to do. Nor can we blame someone else when the results are not topnotch.

We are challenged to make the teaching and training of our children a top priority in our lives. "These commandments that I give you today are to be upon your hearts. Impress them on your children. Talk about them when you sit at home and when you walk along the road, when you lie down and when you get up" (Deuteronomy 6:6-7).

The third assumption is that *Christian educators, wherever they serve, have an obligation to work with their colleagues, both Christian and non-Christian, for their own edification as well as the good of the children they teach.* We have much to learn from one another about education! "Who is wise and understanding among you? Let him show it by his good life, by deeds done in the humility that comes from wisdom. But if you harbor bitter envy and selfish ambition in your hearts, do not boast about it or deny the truth . . . For where you have envy and selfish ambition, there you find disorder and every evil practice. But the wisdom that comes from heaven is first of all pure, then peace-loving, considerate, submissive, full of mercy and good fruit, impartial and sincere" (James 3:13-14, 16-17).

The fourth and final assumption is that *the needs of the total child should be considered when making a schooling decision—spiritual, academic, emotional, psychological, and physical.* While both Ephesians 6 and Colossians 3 tell children to obey and honor their parents ("You'll do what I tell you to do"), Paul also reminds fathers (and mothers) in both books that provoking their offspring can lead to discouragement and anger ("I'm a person too, Dad.") We must listen to what our children are telling us. A schooling decision that does not take the child's needs into consideration is not a good one.

Maybe you're wondering what all the excitement is about. Is school really that important? The answer is yes. Your child (if taught in a formal setting) will spend over 13,000 hours in the process of being "educated." He will spend thirteen years, more than 10% of his life, listening to teachers, reading books, making friends, doing assignments, and (hopefully) learning. This process will affect in a large measure how and what he learns, the ideas and beliefs that he values, who his friends are, and probably, most important of all, his own feelings of self-worth. Schooling decisions are important ones.

The following six-step process will help you make the best schooling choice for your child. The process can be used to make an initial choice as your child begins his or her school career or at any point along the way when a change might be needed—elementary through high school.

- Determine what you believe the role of schooling should be in your child's life.

- Consider your child and his or her special needs, interests, and talents.

- Enumerate your own specific gifts and talents as a parent to determine the part you can play in your child's education.

- Understand the advantages and disadvantages of each schooling option.

- Look at the specific options available to you and make a decision.

- Monitor and evaluate your child's schooling progress.

Step One

Determine what you believe the role of schooling should be in your child's life

Chapter Two will begin to help you determine what you believe about the role of education in your child's life. Is the purpose of education to foster a love for learning and an inquisitive mind? Should schooling prepare young people for the world of work or just teach them facts? As a first step in understanding what you believe about education, complete the Family Education Profile Questionnaire. Knowing what you believe is essential to making a wise schooling choice for your child.

Step Two

Consider your child and his or her special needs, interests, and talents

Some children are adaptable, flexible, and amenable. They fit in anywhere. They get along with everyone. Their abilities are average. Their dispositions are normal. Other children are difficult, challenging, and loud. They push the limits, think rules were made for others, and can't sit still. Some children know it all before you teach it. Others still don't know it after a dozen lessons. Some children learn best from the printed page. Others learn best by touching, talking, and moving. Some children get along well with adults. Some children get along well with children. Some children don't seem to get along well with anyone.

Parents are exposed to a relatively small sample of children—their own. But professionals who work with hundreds of children throughout their careers know how few children are actually "average." Each one has his own unique qualities and characteristics. Every child is special. Understanding your own offspring's strengths and weaknesses will help you evaluate which schooling option will work best. Chapter Three will present several ways in which you can look at your individual child and understand his learning style, personality type, and special gifts and talents.

Step Three

Enumerate your own specific gifts and talents
In addition to understanding what makes your child unique, you need to be practical and reasonable in determining which option will mesh with your own specific gifts and talents. Completing The Parent Profile found in Chapter Four will help you do just that.

Step Four

Understand the advantages and disadvantages of each schooling option
Most of us feel that we understand the schooling process because we once went to school. But we may have a rather one-sided view that could be enlarged by examining the pros and cons of other options. In Chapters Five,

Six, and Seven, we will look at the specific advantages and disadvantages of three different schooling choices: public, Christian, and home schools. Having an overview of each option before you begin to narrow your choices will improve your decision-making process. In addition to the advantages and disadvantages of each schooling option, you'll also be given a list of books and organizations that can provide further information as you make your decision. Finally, each chapter (Five through Seven) will include practical suggestions for implementing that choice.

Step Five

Look at the specific options open to you and make a decision

Once you understand the strengths and weaknesses of each school option, you'll be ready to do an in-depth evaluation of *your* specific choice. Chapter Eight will provide checklists designed to evaluate each option. You'll be able to visit a specific school or examine alternative home-schooling formats to determine which one best meets the needs of your family. Any of the choices in the abstract may appear to be perfectly suited to your child, but once you visit the actual school or do a pilot home-school program, your evaluation may tell you something quite different. Your goal is to make an informed decision.

Step Six

Monitor and evaluate your child's schooling progress

Once you've made your schooling decision, you must pay close attention to your child's progress and be ready to fine-tune and make adjustments along the way. The expectation that you and your child will always be thoroughly happy about every aspect of school is unrealistic. Sometimes you will be dissatisfied. Sometimes your child will be unhappy. And there may be occasions along the way when even the school is displeased. If problems arise at any time in your child's schooling experience, you must be ready to work cooperatively on solutions. Chapter Nine helps parents who are unhappy with their current schooling choice and want to change. It includes stories of families who have made successful transitions to another school setting and offers suggestions to help you decide if a change is really what you need.

Schooling Options: Choosing the Best for You and Your Child is designed to help you make the best possible choice for your child. Read it thoughtfully and prayerfully.

2

The Purpose of Education

Whoso neglects learning in his youth,
Loses the past and is dead for the future.
EURIPIDES

*E*ach September I watch the mothers and fathers of kindergartners as they eagerly bring their offspring to school for the first time. I eavesdrop on their conversations and I can tell from what they are saying what they believe about the purpose of schooling.

- "I sure hope you can straighten him out—he's a holy terror."

- "I need to schedule Johnny into the morning class. It's the only way I can keep my job."

- "Do you have a gifted program in kindergarten?"

- "Here's where you're going to learn to read, Jeremy."

- "Look at all the nice boys and girls. You're going to make lots of friends in kindergarten."

Each of us has different expectations about what the schooling process should do for our children. Step One in determining which schooling choice is best for your family is figuring out what *you* believe the purpose of schooling should be in your child's life. You will in essence be developing your own philosophy of education. Is school just someplace where kids go until they're old enough to be on their own? Some parents think so. They can't wait to get them out of the house and they don't care what happens once they leave. Other parents are totally consumed with early learning. They are enrolling their children in academic preschools at the tender ages of two and three. Still other parents believe that the purpose of schooling is to prepare kids for better job opportunities so they can achieve financial security and status. They examine every course offering with a view to how it might contribute to their child's future success. Others want education to prepare their children to serve their fellow human beings and make a contribution to society. And there are even a few parents left who want their children to develop a love of learning for its own sake. Christian parents want even more from schooling. They want the religious and moral values of the home to be taught and reinforced at school.

◆

Parents are the first and most important of their children's educators.
Universal Declaration of Human Rights, the *United Nations Charter*

No matter which schooling choice you make, however, you as a parent are ultimately responsible for the implementation of your educational philosophy. Whatever you believe should be taught, whether it be American history, teamwork, apologetics, or computer science, *you* are responsible for either teaching the lessons at home or making sure your children learn them someplace else. If you believe that your child should be well grounded in biblical knowledge, then if you're not teaching it at home, you'd better make sure he's learning it elsewhere. If you want your child to be mathematically literate, it generally doesn't happen by osmosis.

Developing your family educational philosophy is an important activity because it will help you articulate what you believe about children, about what they should learn, and about how and where those lessons should be taught.

◆

We learn to do something by doing it. There is no other way. When we first do something, we probably will not do it well. But if we keep on doing it, have good models to follow and helpful advice if and when we feel we need it, and always do it as well as we can, we will do it better. In time, we may do it very well. This process never ends. In that sense, people never stop "learning to do" what they know how to do, no matter how well they do it. They must "learn" every day to do it as well as they can, or they will soon do it less well.

JOHN HOLT, *Instead of Education: Ways to Help People Do Things Better*

Let's begin by looking at three different educational philosophies, one from each of the schooling options. They have some things in common, but they are very different. Reading them will help you determine critical differences between public, Christian, and home schooling. And there *are* some very critical differences.

Public School Philosophy of Education

Democracy requires an educated citizenry. Our society is committed to the education of all people. Since each citizen is an individual of importance and worth, each should have an equal opportunity for self-development. Education is both a right and a privilege. Every citizen has the responsibility to uphold and to build upon his educational heritage. Acceptance of responsibility is imperative if democracy is to operate effectively and if the right and privilege is to be maintained.[1]

Christian School Philosophy of Education

The educational philsophy of Dayton Christian is based on a God-centered view of truth and man as presented in the Bible. Since God created and sustains all things through his Son, Jesus Christ, the universe and all life are dynamically related to God and have the purpose of glorifying him. This is pointedly true of man who was made in God's image, different in kind from all other creation, with the unique capacity to know and respond to God personally and voluntarily. Because man is a sinner by nature and choice, however, he cannot, in this condition, know or honor God in his life. He can do this only by being born again through receiving Jesus Christ as Saviour and Lord, and thus be enabled to do God's will, which is the ultimate purpose of this life.[2]

Home-School Philosophy of Education

We believe children are created by God and belong to him. He places them in families for care and nurturing. We believe our children are a heritage from the Lord and a blessing to our lives. We believe that we as parents are ultimately responsible for the education of our children. We are responsible for selecting and directing their learning experiences. We believe that children are better able to learn when they have the physical or mental capability to perform tasks related to what they are to learn. We believe that each child is a unique individual and, therefore, his education should accomodate that uniqueness.[3]

Possible Educational Goals

Now that you've examined the three philosophies, your next step in the process of developing your own personal philosophy is to consider some specific goals of education. The following list covers many long-range goals that could be accomplished over the twelve or thirteen years of a child's educational experience. Few, if any, will be accomplished in six easy lessons. So don't get excited if your seven-year-old hasn't yet mastered the list. Some of the goals relate specifically to academic content. Others deal with personal growth and development in the spiritual, emotional, and psychological areas. Pay attention to the ones that you think are most important. They will become the foundation of your own philosophy of education.

◆

We should want every student to know how mountains are made, and that for most actions there is an equal and opposite reaction. They should know who said "I am the state" and who said "I have a dream." They should know about subjects and predicates, about isosceles triangles and ellipses. They should know where the Amazon flows and what the First Amendment means. They should know about the Donner Party and slavery, and Shylock, Hercules, and Abigail Adams, where Ethiopia is, and why there is a Berlin Wall . . .

WILLIAM J. BENNETT, former secretary of education, *First Lessons: A Report on Elementary Education in America*

You also need to keep in mind that children begin learning all of these things the moment they are born. Learning self-discipline or how to study God's Word aren't suddenly important when a child turns five. The first three years are especially critical ones for development in all areas—intellectual, spiritual, social, emotional, and physical. I've made this very important point in everything I've written.[4] Parents who let this time slip by lose out on important learning opportunities. Schooling begins at birth. The formal schooling that begins at age five, whether it be public, Christian, or home, can only be as effective as what has happened in the home up to that point, and in what happens in the home once the formal process has begun.

◆

You know that you cannot confidently launch your children into today's world unless they are of strong character and well-educated in the use of language, science, and mathematics. They must possess a deep respect for intelligence, achievement, and learning and the skills needed to use them; for setting goals; and for disciplined work. That respect must be accompanied by an intolerance for the

shoddy and second-rate masquerading as "good enough."
National Commission on Excellence in Education, *A Nation at Risk*

As you read through the goals in the following list (which is by no means complete), think about how important each goal is to you as a parent. Give each goal a rating from 1-5. A high rating means you think the goal is very important and should definitely be an educational outcome. A low rating means that the goal is relatively unimportant to you in your child's overall educational program.

Family Education Profile Questionnaire

____ 1. To develop a growing relationship with God.
____ 2. To have a feeling of self-worth.
____ 3. To learn self-confidence.
____ 4. To become a better citizen.
____ 5. To learn to read with understanding.
____ 6. To become self-reliant and self-sufficient.
____ 7. To learn mathematical skills and principles.
____ 8. To learn self-discipline.
____ 9. To learn how to study God's Word.
____10. To know the will of God and obey it.
____11. To learn good study skills.
____12. To learn problem-solving skills.
____13. To learn to think critically and ask meaningful questions.
____14. To develop a God-centered life view.
____15. To develop perseverance.

_____16. To learn how to be a friend and develop a close relationship with someone.

_____17. To learn to live a peaceful life.

_____18. To learn how to play games and sports.

_____19. To learn how to play a musical instrument.

_____20. To learn how to draw and paint.

_____21. To learn to love learning.

_____22. To learn how to research and reason logically from a biblical perspective.

_____23. To learn to be a good citizen through an understanding and appreciation of our Christian and American heritages.

_____24. To be physically fit and develop good health habits.

_____25. To think creatively and critically.

_____26. To understand current affairs.

_____27. To develop an appreciation for God's creation as it is manifested in the disciplines of science.

_____28. To demonstrate initiative.

_____29. To develop leadership abilities.

_____30. To learn social graces and good manners.

_____31. To learn to speak a foreign language.

_____32. To learn how to work with supervision, independently, cooperatively with another person or with a group, in solitude, in an atmosphere where others are doing the same, and in an atmosphere where others are doing different things.

_____33. To read about and appreciate good literature.

_____34. To learn how to serve others.

_____35. To be motivated.

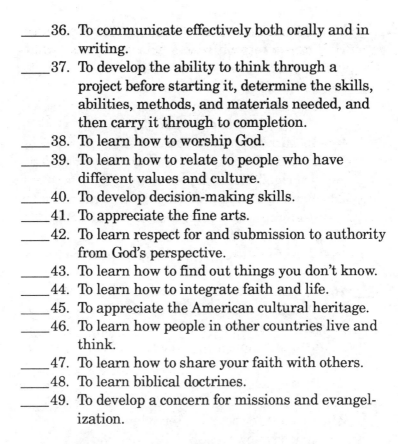

_____36. To communicate effectively both orally and in writing.

_____37. To develop the ability to think through a project before starting it, determine the skills, abilities, methods, and materials needed, and then carry it through to completion.

_____38. To learn how to worship God.

_____39. To learn how to relate to people who have different values and culture.

_____40. To develop decision-making skills.

_____41. To appreciate the fine arts.

_____42. To learn respect for and submission to authority from God's perspective.

_____43. To learn how to find out things you don't know.

_____44. To learn how to integrate faith and life.

_____45. To appreciate the American cultural heritage.

_____46. To learn how people in other countries live and think.

_____47. To learn how to share your faith with others.

_____48. To learn biblical doctrines.

_____49. To develop a concern for missions and evangelization.

Look at the items you have selected as being most important. If you choose the public school setting, there are clearly some educational goals for which you will have complete responsibility at home. (Items number 1, 9, 14, 23, 38, 48, and 49). The public school curriculum will not teach respect for and submission to authority from God's perspective. In fact, in the views of many, it may even undermine respect for and submission to authority from God's perspective. As parents you'll have to teach those lessons at home. The lines of responsibility are firmly drawn between what you have to do and what the public school will do.

◆

Every educational system has a moral goal that it tries to attain and that informs its curriculum. It wants to produce a certain kind of human being. Democratic education, whether it admits it or not, wants and needs to produce men and women who have the tastes, knowledge, and character supportive of a democratic regime.
ALAN BLOOM, *The Closing of the American Mind*

If you choose the Christian school, the lines of responsibility are much more vague. Can you assume that all of the spiritual goals will be covered adequately? Can you relax your vigil and not worry about the spiritual education of your children if they are enrolled in the Christian school? Probably not, although many parents choose the Christian school to back up any weaknesses at home.

> Wisdom is supreme; therefore get wisdom.
> Though it cost all you have, get understanding.
> *Proverbs 4:7*

If you choose to home-school your child, there will be no confusion about who does what. The responsibility is all yours. And you can tell from the list that it is a big one.

Listen, my son, to your father's instruction
and do not forsake your mother's teaching.
They will be a garland to grace your head
and a chain to adorn your neck.

Proverbs 1: 8-9

Now take a few minutes to jot down answers to the following questions. This process should further direct your thinking as you contemplate the best schooling choice for your child.

- Who is ultimately responsible for your children's educational experiences?

- What do you want more than anything for your children?

- Where should schooling take place?

- What are the best teaching methods for young children, middle-graders, adolescents?

- What role does social development play in learning?

- What principles should guide the choices of books and other learning materials?

- How important is discipline in the educational process?

- Is there any limit to what your child can learn?

- What's more important—"book learning" or "practical knowledge"?

- Is there any such thing as a child who can't learn?

- Should children be expected to enjoy learning for its own sake or do they need rewards and incentives?

- When does education begin?

Usually when authors pose questions, they also supply answers. But that is not the purpose of this chapter. Its purpose is to get you thinking about what *you* believe. Continue to think about those beliefs as you read the remaining chapters. This is not a book about the "right" schooling choice, but a book about the "best" schooling choice for *your* family.

> In my dealing with my child, my Latin and Greek, my accomplishments and my money stead me nothing; but as much soul as I have avails.
> RALPH WALDO EMERSON

The answers are not always easy ones. Sometimes people deeply want their children to attend the Christian school. They place them there, believing it is the right choice, but their kids are miserable and unhappy.

Sometimes parents would love to home-school their children, but they have to work outside the home. There are parents who believe the public schools are an important area of ministry, but don't want to see their children corrupted by the evil influences they see there. And there are loads of people who made a choice, have never regretted it, whose kids have turned out well. In my interviews with dozens of public, Christian, and home-school parents, I have found happy and unhappy parents in every setting. How to school your children is often a difficult decision, but you've made the first step—deciding what you believe about the purpose of education.

If you think one year ahead—sow a seed.
If you think ten years ahead—plant a tree.
If you think a hundred years ahead—educate the people.
CHINESE PROVERB

3

What's Best for
Your Child?

Your children are not yours.
KAHLIL GIBRAN

Step Two in choosing a schooling option for your child is to consider the child and what might be best for him or her. Some parents may object to considering what the child needs. After all, they argue, parents are charged with the educational responsibility and they know what's best for their children, don't they? However, when it comes right down to it, many parents don't know their children all that well. Oh yes, they may know that Susie loves bubble gum ice cream or that Johnny never eats a hot dog with a bun. But when it comes to questions of learning style, unique strengths and weaknesses, or even which areas of special intelligence their child has, most parents are woefully uninformed. They fail to see their child as a wonderful God-given creation who is totally different from any other child. They sometimes don't even appreciate the special gifts and talents their child actually has. All they can see is what their child isn't.

In this chapter we will examine several different models or ways of looking at your child. They are all manmade creations, but each will give you a slightly different framework for understanding your child and what he or she can become. However, simply knowing the information is not enough. It must be used in the context of educational choices and in helping you determine what avenue is best for your child.

Your Child's Unique Design

◆

When the teacher begins to view each student as having a certain type of personality and a particular learning pattern he will no longer expect all students to be responsive to the same educational program. Nor will he attempt to teach each student individually. Once a student's learning pattern is identified, the teacher can group students according to their similar learning patterns and teach students within each group via the same instructional methods and materials.
KEITH GOLAY, *Learning Patterns & Temperament Styles*

In *Discovering Your Child's Design,* Ralph Mattson and Thom Black hypothesize that each child has a unique design, which can be uncovered with some skillful detective work by the parent. They suggest that if we as parents understand our child's design, we can parent at an optimum level. We will be able to "enhance development, affirm uniqueness, appreciate individuality, cultivate appropriate play opportunities, encourage a fitting social style, facilitate formal learning, enhance problem solving, and provide effective career counseling."[1]

The authors also suggest keeping a Design Journal in which you closely observe your child over a period of time and for each observation record the following things: the specific action a child takes, significant quotes from any conversation that takes place with others during the observation, quotes from interviewing the child subsequent to an observation, and preliminary ideas about what you see. These observations will vary greatly with the age of the child, but the format is applicable to both toddlers and teen-agers.

Mattson and Black warn that even among the most sensitive and caring parents there is a tendency to encourage only the behaviors they want to see in their child or even to try to force a child into a mold for which he or she is miscast.

They suggest considering what your child chooses to do when he or she has a choice, not what you would *prefer* he or she do based on *your* interests. They offer six questions to help you find out.

1. Is your child pushed or pulled into action (by outside influences or from within)?

2. What specifically pushes or pulls ̣ ity, peers, leader)?

3. How much time does your child use to complete a task (a little, a moderate amount, or a lot)?

4. To what kind of environment is your child drawn (inside, outside, strange places, familiar ones)?

5. What does your child like to encounter (problems, information, friends, a challenge, applause, conflict)?

6. What capabilities does your child consistently use (visual, audio, oral, mechanical, manual or physical, intellectual/mental, leadership)?[2]

Mattson and Black believe that if you watch your child over an extended period of time, you will begin to see a pattern emerge; they call it your child's "design." This "design" will serve as a guide for you as you make life choices for your child—including which mode of schooling to pursue.

Special Intelligence

◆

The modern school (both Christian and public) has a very narrow focus on logical, problem-solving abilities and verbal intelligence. Students who are naturally drawn to this emphasis can do very well and will be strongly affirmed by the reward systems of the school. But students whose inherent strengths find no natural expression in the structure of the school system will wonder about their value as persons. The best things they have to offer—the very gifts for which God has designed them—are no more than casually appreciated.

RALPH MATTSON and THOM BLACK, *Discovering Your Child's Design*

In addition to determining your child's unique design, there is a second way of looking at him or her—determining which kinds of special intelligences he or she has. Most people understand intelligence in terms of a rather narrow ability to do well on an intelligence test. But Howard Gardner, a Harvard psychologist, hypothesizes seven different kinds of intelligence located in different parts of the brain: *Linguistic, Logical-Mathematical, Spatial, Musical, Bodily Kinesthetic, Interpersonal,* and *Intrapersonal.*[3] His theory gives us another way to look at the gifts and talents of our children. *Linguistic intelligence* is centered in language. Readers, writers, and storytellers are all linguistically gifted. Children with these gifts like to write, read, spell, do crossword puzzles, and play word games. Individuals with the second kind of intelligence—*logical-mathematical*—think conceptually. They love figuring out the answers to difficult problems and most likely are very logical thinkers. Children with strengths in this area like computers, chess, checkers, strategy games, and puzzles.

Spatially intelligent people think in images and pictures. They can draw, design, and visualize the way a room will look with new furniture and wallpaper. Children with strengths in this area spend a lot of time in art-related activities. *Musical* and *bodily-kinesthestic intelligences*, the fourth and fifth varieties, result in expertise in the areas of performing and composing music, sports, and physical activities. And finally, there are two areas that are especially interesting since they hypothesize types of intelligence that we frequently overlook in people—*interpersonal* and *intrapersonal*. Children with *interpersonal intelligence* understand other people. They are the leaders and communicators. The student council president or the kid that everybody likes probably has a high level of *interpersonal intelligence. Intrapersonal intelligence* is just the opposite. Individuals with this quality are very independent. They rely on their own judgment, have a deep sense of self-confidence, and generally don't care what everyone else is wearing or doing. They have their own agenda. Keep in mind that individuals can have several different kinds of intelligence and in varying amounts or degrees. The practical applications of Gardner's theory have been developed by Thomas Armstrong in the book, *In Their Own Way: Discovering and Encouraging Your Child's Personal Learning Style.*

Learning Styles

We are God's workmanship, created in Christ Jesus to do good works, which God prepared in advance for us to do.

Ephesians 2:10

A third way of looking at your child is to try to figure out what learning style he or she favors. The simplest way is to consider the three basic types of learning: *visual, auditory,* and *kinesthetic.* A *visual learner* learns best by seeing, an *auditory learner* by hearing, and a *kinesthetic learner* by touching.

If your child loves to listen to stories for hours on end, then chances are he's an *auditory learner*. He can probably understand and remember material better if he hears it. On the other hand, if your little darling has to touch everything in sight, take it apart and see how it works, she's probably a *kinesthetic learner*. She may have a difficult time sitting still in class and doing paper and pencil tasks. The *visual learner* will notice small details about what people are wearing or what has happened. The *visual learner* needs to see something written down or illustrated before he can remember it.

These learning preferences will determine what kinds of learning activities will work best for your child. Many children can move easily between the learning styles, but a child with a very strong predominant style may have a problem adapting. Ideally, we want children to be able to learn using all of these styles, but when a child is having difficulty, knowing his preferred learning style will help us pick the best learning environment.

Left-Brained or Right-Brained?

Another way of looking at how children learn is through brain hemisphericity. While we all use both hemispheres of our brain, it's helpful for parents to understand which

31

thinking or reasoning patterns characterize each hemisphere, along with the related school skills. Primarily left-brained individuals do their processing (thinking or reasoning) in an analytical-sequential fashion. They prefer verbal explanations, use language to remember, produce ideas logically, like structured experiences, and approach problems seriously.[4] The school skills that relate to this type of processing are symbols, language, reading, phonics, locating details and facts, talking and reciting, following directions, listening, and auditory association.[5] Left-brained individuals just naturally relate to the ways most conventional schools are structured.

Individuals who are primarily right-brained do their processing in a wholistic-simultaneous way. They prefer visual explanations, use images to remember, produce ideas intuitively, prefer abstract thinking tasks, like open fluid experiences, and approach problems playfully.[6] School skills that use this type of processing are those that deal with spatial relationships, mathematical concepts, color sensitivity, singing and music, art expression, creativity, and visualization.[7] Strongly right-brained individuals frequently have problems coping with the structure of most school classrooms. They have alternate ways of learning that conventionally trained teachers sometimes have a difficult time tapping.

Learning Patterns and Temperaments

Organize your energies along your own line of natural interest and persistence, and you will do more, much more, so much better.
GEORG KAISER

Dr. Keith Golay has developed yet another way of looking at your child's learning patterns and temperaments.[8] He suggests four categories: *actual-spontaneous, actual-routine, conceptual-specific,* and *conceptual-global.*

Children who are described as *actual-spontaneous* are hands-on, active learners. They don't have time to go through the planning and organizing stages of a project. They want to jump right in and do it. They want things to move quickly and be active. Art, music, and physical education are their favorite subjects. They hate homework and can't stand anyone telling them what to do. The *actual-spontaneous* learner despises the structure of school and can't wait to get out of the classroom. He needs tasks that involve manipulating, constructing, and operating to be truly fulfilled.

Actual-routine children are perfect students. Their desks are well organized. They love the systems of school—the rules, the routine, and the memorization and drill. They have to be forced to break out of their molds to try creative writing, drama, or role playing. Just give the *actual-routine* child a workbook and he or she will be happy all day. The *actual-routine* child loves helping the teacher and can be found after school emptying wastebaskets or cleaning the blackboard.

The third type of learner is *conceptual-specific*. These children aren't as social as they probably should be. They get impatient when other people don't understand as quickly as they do. They like math, science, engineering, and problem solving. They find group discussions a waste of time and resent the constant repetition of previously mastered material. They have an insatiable desire to learn and pick up information in an effortless way. They are frequently seen by their peers as "different." Unless guided toward appropriate social graces, the *conceptual-specific* child can become an isolate.

The fourth and final category, *conceptual-global,* contains children who do well in school, but thrive on cooperation rather than competition. These children prefer the humanities rather than the sciences and enjoy group discussions, role playing, and the good feeling that comes from making a contribution to a group. The *conceptual-global* child is a "people person" and seems to have an innate sense of how to get along with others. Friends frequently seek him out for assistance and advice.

Your Learning Style vs. Your Child's

Bernice McCarthy, author of the 4Mat system, another model for looking at learning styles, warns parents whose personal learning styles are drastically different from that of their children to be careful when they are doing the teaching. Major squabbles can ensue when parent/child learning styles clash. McCarthy has developed four style categories: *innovative, analytic, commonsense,* and *dynamic.*[9]

Innovative children learn by listening to others and sharing ideas. They start with what they see and then generalize. They enjoy small-group interaction, role playing, team sports, and simulation, but they don't like timed tests, debates, and computer-assisted instruction.

They want to know how things directly affect the lives of those around them.

Analytic learners enjoy listening to the teacher lecture. They are thinkers and watchers with rational and sequential thinking patterns. They enjoy programmed instruction, well-organized lectures or stories, competition, demonstration, and objective tests, but dislike role play, open discussion, and group projects. They want realistic and practical information and tend to be perfectionistic.

Students with the *commonsense style* enjoy problem solving, debates, logic problems, independent study, and especially experiments that build on what they have learned. They do not value input while they are trying things out. They dislike memorizing, a lot of reading, group work, and writing assignments. They need to be challenged to check the validity of their knowledge. They want to discover how things work and how they can be applied to real life. They may be mislabeled as "hyperactive" but will respond to a teacher who is an intellectual challenger and fellow learner and who is logical and just.

Dynamic children like to see, hear, touch, and feel. They get bored easily unless they can learn by trial and error, taking action, and carrying out plans. They enjoy case studies, guided imagery, drama, creative productions, and assignments that require originality. They dislike assignments without options, standard routines, or activities done in haste. They want a teacher who is a facilitator and stimulator of ideas and who is curious and imaginative, encouraging them to explore the possibilities of what is known.

Your Child's Temperament

◆

> Students who do well on a task feel good about the task, the school, the teacher and themselves. In discovering that they are good students, they learn that they have value in the eyes of teachers, parents and even other students. Students who do poorly on a task feel unhappy about the task and everything associated with it, including themselves. Bad students learn that they are bad people.
>
> PAUL CHANCE, "Master of Mastery" in *Psychology Today*

Discovering your child's unique design, figuring out what special types of intelligence he has, or figuring how she learns aren't the only ways you can study your child. Children also come in a variety of temperaments. Drs. Alexander Thomas and Stella Chess have advanced the theory that a child's temperament plays a big part in determining the development of his personality. They studied a total of 141 middle- and upper-middle-class children, 95 children from working class Puerto Rican families, a small sample of children from an Israeli kibbutz, 68 children born prematurely, and 243 children with congenital rubella. In all of the groups, three definite temperaments were identified: the *Easy Child,* the *Difficult Child,* and the *Slow-to-Warm-Up Child.*[10]

The *Easy Child* is characterized by regularity, positive approach to new stimuli, high adaptability to change, and a mild or moderately intense mood that is usually positive. These children develop regular sleep and feeding schedules, take to most new foods easily, smile at strangers, adapt easily to a new school, accept most frustration with little fuss, and accept the rules of new games with no trouble. This type of child is well liked by his parents, his pediatrician, and his teachers. After an easy infancy, he goes on to sail through life.

The *Difficult Child,* through no fault of his own, is at the opposite end of the continuum. He is irregular in both his feeding and sleeping schedules, takes a long time to adjust to anything new, and spends a lot of time crying when he is a newborn. Frustration results in tantrums and the *Difficult Child* makes everyone around him wonder what they're doing wrong. The *Difficult Child* can outgrow many of his "prickly" habits, but he takes much patience and love.

The *Slow-to-Warm-Up Child* is somewhere in the middle. Even though she may react negatively to a new situation, once she's had a chance to check things out, she usually comes around.

Understanding Your Child

I praise you because I am fearfully and wonderfully made; your works are wonderful, I know that full well.
Psalm 139:14

Maybe you're asking yourself, "What difference does all of this make, anyway? So what if my child is a kinesthetic, analytic, conceptual-global, with extraordinary amounts of spatial and interpersonal intelligence and a slow-to-warm-up temperament? What do I do tomorrow?"

The point of this chapter is not necessarily to help you figure out today exactly what your child is or isn't. If you're interested in a specific author's ideas, you can find the volumes mentioned and pursue the subject in more depth. You probably won't be able to handle more than one model at a time or you'll become totally confused. What I do hope you have begun to do is think of your child as a unique learner whose needs might better be met in one setting over another. A child who likes routine, drill, memorization, and structure will thrive in a programmed learning workbook or a tightly controlled classroom setting. The dynamic, simultaneous learner, on the other hand, will do better with an off-the-wall teacher who is totally unpredictable and slightly zany. The child who has strong leadership abilities and needs lots of group interaction and relationships with other adults and children will probably be bored stiff at home with just his mother. He will crave the action and excitement of the school playground. The child with a high degree of spatial intelligence will do much better at home where she can play games, do problems in her head, and design her own projects and lessons.

Understanding your child's strengths and how he/she learns will not only help you come up with the best schooling choice for now, it will help you get the most you can out of that choice in the years to come. Just because everyone in your family for the past six generations has gone to the Christian school doesn't mean it's necessarily the right choice for your child. Think about how he will fit in with that educational program. Even if all of your friends are raving about the advantages of home schooling, that doesn't guarantee that you and your little darling won't be at each other's throats by October. Nor are there any guarantees that the highly acclaimed public school that's right across the streeet will be exactly right for your child.

In Chapters One and Two you've considered your philosophy of education. Now you have a clear understanding of your child and his unique characteristics as a learner. But what about you as a parent? The following chapter will help you examine which schooling choice is best suited to you.

4

Your Part
as Parent

*If you affirm and believe in your children, you will get it
back, no matter where they go to school.*
ANONYMOUS

Sally home-schools her children. Although not an educator by training, she reads voraciously about teaching
and learning. She has collected dozens of books, keeps a
clipping file of home-schooling materials, and subscribes
to several newsletters. Once or twice a year she attends
a convention or home-schooling workshop. She and her
husband, Rich, buy whatever is needed to provide materials and equipment for their home school. They are
deeply committed to their three children, Jason, Jen-
nifer, and Justin. "The three J's," as their parents call
them, are each very different, but they do share one
thing in common—good study habits and a love of learning. Sally's life is built around them and she seldom takes

a break from the work of home schooling. Even in the summer, learning goes on. She believes that the sacrifices she has made by putting her career on hold will pay rich dividends as her children reach maturity well-grounded in both academics and in their Christian faith. She has used the home-schooling opportunity to begin a small business in which her children participate. Sally is not particularly involved in her church and community, preferring instead to focus her energies on home schooling. She's not looking forward to the day when her children "leave the nest," but rests secure that she will have done everything possible to launch them well.

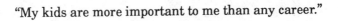

"My kids are more important to me than any career."

Marian is a single parent. She believes that the Christian school is the best supplement to what she believes and teaches at home. Because she is raising her daughter and son alone and works long hours, she feels that the teachers and students at the Christian school will make up for her absence. She is willing to spend whatever it takes to give her children a good education. The teachers take extra time to work with kids who need help and the other students come from Christian homes where parents share Marian's values. Marian can send her children off to school without worrying about what kind of language her daughter, Kathy, will hear on the playground or what kind of textbooks her son, Adam, will encounter in the classroom. Although she doesn't attend the church that sponsors the school, the theology is close enough to be acceptable to Marian. And even though she drives her kids several miles to school each day and has to pick up friends on weekends for play, she doesn't mind the extra effort. The security she feels in having them protected from what she knows is happening in the public schools more than makes up for it. The Christian school has offered a support system to Marian, giving her a tuition scholarship when money got tight. She relies on the teachers and principal for advice about her children and even took two of her vacation days to help out with a Christmas bazaar. The male principal has been an especially good role model for Adam.

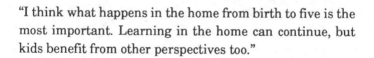

"I think what happens in the home from birth to five is the most important. Learning in the home can continue, but kids benefit from other perspectives too."

Joanie and her husband, Ken, have always had a burden for missions. They attended an inner city church for ten years and chose the public schools because they wanted to continue their outreach. Their last son has just graduated from high school and their three older children are launched into careers and growing families. They delight in sharing the stories of the friendships and outreach their children have had in the public schools, and the ways they've used course assignments to enlarge their ministry. Their home has always been open to a variety of strange and wonderful high-school students with jean jackets and outrageous T-shirts. They seem unworried by the possibility of their children being exposed to unhealthy influences. Joanie has a career as an advertising executive and has worked since her last son started first grade. She was always aware of what was going on at school, but didn't have time to run for PTA offices or volunteer in the library. Joanie and Ken believe they have more to learn from their children than their children have to learn from them and have an unusual confidence in their children's ability to make good decisions and moral judgments. Their children are committed Christians, and one is training for the mission field.

◆

"When do we start trusting our kids and letting them go?"

Sally, Rich, Marian, Joanie, and Ken are composites of the dozens of people I interviewed during the writing of this book. Perhaps you will see yourself among their descriptions. And maybe you will also see that all of the school options work well—if you make the right choice.

Your Specific Gifts and Talents as a Parent

After considering your philosophy of education in Chapter Two and your child's talents and gifts in Chapter

Three, it's time for the next step: looking at your own specific gifts and talents as a parent to help determine the role you wish to play in your child's education.

———————◆———————

"The Christian school is the only way. We went to Christian schools and so will our kids and grandkids."

———————————————

Can you afford a Christian school education? As a single parent, do you need the extra Christian influence and role models Christian schools can provide for your children?

———————◆———————

"Home-schooling is a way of life."

———————————————

Do you have the time, energy, and talents to make home schooling work for your children?

Are you committed to being a Christian witness, through prayer and volunteer work, in the public school? Are you willing to take the extra time and guidance needed to help your children make wise decisions about friends, values, and activities in the public school setting?

In order to help you think further about the best schooling choice for you as a parent, complete Part I of The Parent Profile. Part I will help you see whether the *home-schooling* option is a viable one for you.

The Parent Profile, Part I

Answer yes or no to each question.

_____ 1. I want or need to work outside of my home.

_____ 2. I get along well with my children and they generally obey my directives.

_____ 3. I am poorly organized and require deadlines to keep me moving.

_____ 4. There's nothing I like better than doing an art project at the dining-room table.

_____ 5. I tend to give in when my children wheedle and cajole me.

_____ 6. I love to learn new things and can't bear to leave a question unanswered.

_____ 7. I need lots of contact with adults or I get bored.

_____ 8. I am totally committed to my children.

_____ 9. I am rather inflexible and demanding.

_____10. I am a very patient person.

_____11. I feel that I've done all I can for my children and I want someone else to have a turn.

_____12. I want to be intimately involved in every aspect of my child's life.

If you answered yes to the majority of the even-numbered questions, then you're well suited for the home-schooling option. If you answered yes to almost all of the odd-numbered questions, then think about sending your child off to school.

Part II of The Parent Profile will help you decide whether the *Christian* or *public school* option is better suited to you.

The Parent Profile, Part II

Answer yes or no to each question.

____ 1. I feel uncomfortable when I or my children have to spend long periods of time with non-Christians.

____ 2. I can share my faith with others with little difficulty.

____ 3. I worry about the influences of secular texts and library books.

____ 4. I enjoy controversial discussions and like to expose my children to a variety of different ideas and beliefs.

____ 5. I don't believe we are doing enough in our home to teach our children about the Bible.

____ 6. I like to get involved in organizations where I can effect change and influence people for Christ.

____ 7. I'd feel guilty if I didn't send my children to a Christian school.

____ 8. I think Christian schools are often narrow and provincial in their outlook.

____ 9. I believe that Christian teachers can do a better job of teaching than non-Christians.

____10. I can't afford Christian school tuition.

____11. I'm willing to sacrifice and cut back on everything to send my kids to the Christian school.

____12. I think that education and the church should be kept separate.

If you answered yes to almost all of the odd-numbered questions, then the Christian school option is the one for you. If you answered yes to almost all of the even-numbered questions, then you and your family are well suited to public schools.

Questionnaires like the ones you just completed are arbitrary and artificial at best. There are many more factors than can be contained in a few simple yes or no questions. But The Parent Profile can help you begin to understand how your strengths and weaknesses as a parent enter into the schooling decision.

Now let's look at the advantages and disadvantages of each schooling option.

5

Pros and Cons of Public Schooling

*If the battle for the
hearts and minds of our children
is being fought in our public schools, the church must not
abandon those who feel called
to be salt and light in the secular classroom.
The moral development of a generation
will be jeopardized if we do.*
TIMOTHY JONES, Editorial in *Christianity Today*

*P*ublic schools are always in the news. And most of the news is bad, it seems. Discipline, textbooks, academic standards, and drugs are just a few of the issues that concern parents—and not just those who are Christians. A review of titles in the public library will raise your level of concern even higher: *What They Are Doing to Your Children*; *Don't Blame the Kids: The Trouble with America's Public Schools*; *Is Public Education Neces-*

sary? Without a deep look into the public schools, you might be ready to discount them as an option before you even begin your study.

Cliff Schimmels, educator and author, wanted to find out if the horror stories were true. So, in the fall of 1984, he enrolled as an undercover freshman at West Aurora High School. In his words:

> Located along the banks of the Fox River about forty miles from Chicago, Aurora is an old industrial town that is rapidly becoming a suburb. I saw all types of communities: nineteenth-century homes and business buildings replete with history and charm; suburban middle-class development homes, growing out of recently converted cornfields; and high-rise, low-income apartments built for the influx of the city moving out.[1]

Cliff attended school for six weeks, going to a full schedule of classes, socializing with students, and doing his homework. I'm sure his publisher was looking for an exposè filled with horror stories about drugs, violence, and atheism. After all, those are the books that sell! Instead, he produced a positive, upbeat volume that promotes public schools. Cliff tells about speaking to a group of West Aurora parents at the conclusion of his experience:

> I was serious, mixing in just enough humor to keep attention. When I finished, I asked if there were any questions. One man raised his hand with emphasis.
> "Yes, sir?" When men raise their hands with em-

phasis, I call them sir, even now when I am no longer a freshman.

"You paint a rosy picture of that school out there. Now tell us what was negative about it." And he sat back in his chair with a funny half smile on his mouth.

Let's stop here. I don't know what else to say. If the truth of what happened to me at West Aurora High School for six weeks during the fall of 1984 is positive, then let's be positive. Why do we insist on hunting for negatives if we have to hunt for them?

I don't know about any other school in the nation. I don't even know about the other students in other classes at West Aurora, but I do know that those people who were in class with me received the benefits of great teaching and solid education for those six weeks. Maybe now that I am gone, even those teachers have quit working so hard, but I doubt it. If they were just putting on an act for six weeks, they are good actors. After the meeting tonight, one of the school officials told me how I could become rich and famous. "Why don't you write a book about this experience and fill it with horror stories," he said. "That ought to make you a best-seller."[2]

I've talked with Cliff about his speaking experiences since writing the book. "Wherever I go," he says, "many Christians are waiting to bash the public schools. They don't believe that good things can happen for Christians in the public schools." Cliff gives this advice: "If you don't believe me, go into the public schools and see for yourself. Don't believe Phyllis Schafley or Barbara Walters or any of the other 'experts.' "

Public School Advantages

The "salt and light" option

The Tuttles put a swimming pool in their back yard and remodeled their basement into a recreation room. These improvements to their home weren't designed to increase its saleability, but were part of a neighborhood ministry to children.

"We feel if we have a home, it's an extension of our family, a place to minister to others," says Rich Tuttle, youth minister at Grace Fellowship in Stone Mountain, Georgia. "Not only do we want to know where our kids are and who their friends are, but we want to know what's going on in the neighborhood."

He says that having groups of kids over enables the Tuttle family to be a witness both to these children and to their parents. It's also one of the reasons their children attend the local public school. Recently moved to the South from the Chicago area, the Tuttles didn't think twice about enrolling their children in public school. They just looked around for the best one.

"Somewhere, we have to learn to be the 'salt and light,' " emphasizes Rich, "and I feel that our children can best have that opportunity if they are enrolled in the public school."

He recently helped his daughter Stacy research a Bible question that came up as part of a classroom discussion. She returned to her classroom and explained to the teacher what she had found. Further discussions have resulted, and Stacy is experiencing what witnessing is all about.

Kathy Tuttle, a certified dental assistant, works part-time, but is "mostly a housewife." She and Rich together do all they can to teach their children—Stacy, 10, Chantel, 7, and Michelle, 5—at home. They feel that music is an especially important part of a young person's life and have exposed their children to a wide range of Christian music. Books are another important teaching tool in their home.

"Our rule of thumb is you can buy all the books you want," laughs Rich. "We feel that our children need to be exposed to the best in both Christian and secular literature."

The Tuttles know the problems their children face in public school classrooms. But they read the library books along with their children, do homework assignments together, and are in regular contact with the principal and teachers. It's all part of the commitment they have made as a family to witness in their community.

Are there any advantages to attending the public school? David and Donna Brown, missionaries who recently returned to this country from a decade in Japan, think so. Their children have attended Japanese schools, home schools, and Christian schools. They now are happily settled in a neighborhood public school.

Dottie and Mark Williams think so, too. This young professional couple recently transferred their children from a Christian school to the local public school. What advantages do these and other families see in their public school?

Access to special programs
Programs like art, music, physical education, extra-curricular sports and clubs, computers, library learning centers, remedial programs for the learning-disabled,

and opportunities for gifted students are usually more readily available in the public schools. This advantage is a very important one to consider. If your child has an unusual talent or a special need, the public school is often the only place that can meet that need. Steve and Maria Gunther's daughter Amy is in eighth grade and a star basketball player. She spends most of her time shooting baskets in the driveway. Her Christian school class of fifteen contains only seven people who want to play basketball. Six of them are boys and she is the best player among the group. The boys constantly taunt her and the coach is unwilling to let her play competitively. Although her parents were deeply committed to the idea of a Christian school education for their child, Amy's growing unhappiness and the lure of a winning girls' basketball team at the local high school are causing the Gunthers to re-evaluate their position.

While many Christian schools are able to offer some of the special programs listed earlier, rarely are they as comprehensive as those offered in the public schools. The Dixons had a similar experience with their daughter Vicky. She was having a great deal of trouble learning to read and the Christian school's limited resources made special help impossible. Their decision was a difficult one since no one in their family had ever attended the public school. The minute Vicky enrolled in the public school she was diagnosed with a learning disability and spent two years in a resource program. She is now reading above grade level and has exited the special program. Her parents are ecstatic. Successes like Vicky's are not always the norm, but for the Dixons, the extra services of the public school were a necessity.

Low cost

◆

> Within the next five years, more than half the states will allow parents to look beyond their own district in choosing which school they want their children to attend.
> NANCY HENDERSON, "Sizing Up Your Local School" in *Changing Times*

As I write out a check for my son's registration fees, I remark to a friend that a free public education is a myth. There are towel and locker fees, book rental, charges for extracurricular activities and sports, and even a fee for an identification card. Compared, however, to the check for tuition that my friend will write to the local Christian high school, my outlay is small. Parents who enroll their children in public schools pay for their education only once, at tax time. Although many parents testify to the provision of God in their lives when they stretch the budget to send their children to Christian schools, many families simply cannot afford it, particularly single parents and parents with several children.

Social opportunities with neighborhood friends
Attending a school that is different from his or her neighborhood friends certainly doesn't eliminate social opportunities for your child. However, if your child is home-schooled or attends Christian school outside of your neighborhood, you will need to spend more time

arranging "social" events and structuring play opportunities than if your child attends school with his neighborhood peers.

◆

I believe I have a responsibility both as a Christian and as an American citizen to support and influence the public schools. I believe also that in the majority of circumstances children from godly homes and Christ-honoring churches will function well in the public school arena.

DAVID SMITH in *Schooling Choices: An Examination of Private, Public & Home Education*

Opportunity to know children from a broad cross section of society

This particular advantage will depend largely on the school your children attend. If your neighborhood school enrolls children from a variety of ethnic, socio-economic, and religious backgrounds, your child will enjoy the rich experience of knowing students from every walk of life. One parent I interviewed compared her experiences as a high-schooler in a sheltered situation to those of her children, attending a school with a high minority population. "My kids have friends of all varieties. But they have a much healthier reality about those friends. They don't have the 'us-them' attitude that took me years to overcome." Depending on your choice of public school, however, the student population may be more homogeneous than the Christian school.

Opportunity to "practice" Christian living in a "real-world" setting

◆

Rather than continue to bemoan the demise of public education in this country, each of us as Christians should "gird up our loins" and utilize the power and odds which God has so abundantly made available to us. Jesus touched upon the necessity of using the resources God has given us when he said: "You are the world's light—a city on a hill, glowing in the night for all to see. Don't hide your light! Let it shine for all; let your good deeds glow for all to see, so that they will praise your heavenly Father" (Matthew 5:14-16, *The Living Bible*).

JON BARTON and JOHN WHITEHEAD, *Schools on Fire: It's Not Too Late to Save the Public Schools*

This is one of the most hotly debated advantages of attending the public school. Christian and home-school advocates consistently point out the dangers of sending "tender plants" out of the greenhouse too early before they have matured. They warn parents that the temptations and pressures of the public school environment will retard the growth and development of even the hardiest of "plants."

But many of the parents I interviewed found these experiences in the real world to be "builders of character and faith." "There's a healthier reality about what's really dangerous when your child is out in the real world," explained one parent. "In the Christian community, it's hard to know who's really committed and who's just pretending." When Christian students in the public school take a stand like Nancy Bushy and her friends from Downers Grove, Illinois, their testimony makes the news. These eager high-schoolers organized a community-based religious service to commemorate their graduation when administrators from two high schools cancelled the traditional baccalaureate service "for lack of interest."

Opportunity for parents to make a positive impact on the school and community

Visalia, California pastor Wayne Jacobsen and his wife are deeply involved in the public schools. They didn't just send their children off to school. "We had to go there ourselves, helping out where we could, making those schools better places for our children and their classmates." The Jacobsens were involved in PTA leadership, classroom volunteering, and parent-teacher advisory committee meetings.

Donna Brown has served for two years as PTA president and volunteers weekly in the school library. She and a group of community women meet weekly to pray for public school principals, teachers, and students.

Other parents run for the school board. Kathleen Cruse is such a parent. Dismayed over the choice of reading materials for junior-high-school students in her district, she decided to get involved. A shy and soft-spoken individual, Kathleen originally tried to find someone else to run. She has never been comfortable in the limelight. But no one was willing. So she gathered her courage, submitted her petitions, and to her surprise was elected. Although her voice is only one among the seven elected board members, she is doing her homework and vows to be a strong conscience for the board as they adopt curriculum materials and approve programs.

Public School Disadvantages

While there are many distinct advantages to be found for students attending the public schools, there are disadvantages as well. Both Dottie Williams and Donna Brown mentioned the high proportion of students from dysfunctional families that take the teacher's time and energy away from children who really want to learn. They also pointed out other problems that keep them ever vigilant as parents of public school students, problems they said they must deal with through extra counseling and teaching at home.

Teachers, students, and the parent community do not necessarily share the Christian values of home
Dottie and Donna were distressed because their children were hearing obscene language from fellow classmates and were being exposed to peer pressure with regard to films and music. On occasion, both moms felt that textbooks and library books have needed further explanation and discussion within the context of a Christian

home. And both believed they needed to monitor their children's friends and be more involved with social activities, since they couldn't always assume their children's choices were good ones.

◆

The public feels the biggest problem facing the public schools today is drug abuse. Prior to 1986, discipline was the biggest concern, but drugs has held the number one spot for the past three years.

STANLEY M. ELAM and ALEC M. GALLUP, "21st Annual Gallup Poll of the Public's Attitudes Toward the Public Schools" in *Phi Delta Kappan*

Some public schools are poorly staffed and administered, particularly in urban or rural areas

The Chicago Public Schools are perhaps the best (or worst) example of an urban school system in disarray. Former Secretary of Education William Bennett called it the "worst in America." The *Chicago Tribune* in a 1988 series on the system called it a "disgrace."[3] The charges levied against public education by its most vocal critics, both secular and Christian, were well documented in the newspaper series with vivid examples of moral depravity, drugs, violence, and rock-bottom academics. Apathetic teachers and administrators, illiterate students, a teachers' union with an iron grip on the system, and a bloated bureaucracy have all done their part to bring the system to its knees. Every public school system suffers when one in its number fails in the mission to educate. Parents who live in areas where public schools are failing have few choices, especially if they are poor. The best hope is strong parental involvement and local control.

Parents have little direct control over textbooks, curriculum, educational experiences, and teaching methodology
Texts and materials may present lifestyles, values, and ideas that are in direct conflict with Christian teachings. Secular humanism is often mentioned as the root of many problems in the public school. Paul Kienel, Executive Director of the Association of Christian Schools International, believes that the pervasive humanistic trend is responsible for a decline in respect for authority, self-centeredness, and total academic freedom.[4] And Tim LaHaye, a vigorous critic of the public schools, believes that "secular educators no longer make learning their primary objective." He feels that "our public schools have become conduits to the minds of our youth, training them to be anti-God, antimoral, antifamily, anti-free enterprise and anti-American."[5]

Phyllis Schlafly, in her foreword to *Child Abuse in the Classroom* (a summary of testimony from parents and educators to the U.S. Department of Education on proposed regulations for the Protection of Pupil Rights Amendment), speaks for many parents when she states that "public schools have alienated children from their parents, from traditional morality such as the Ten Commandments, and from our American heritage."[6] The testimony contains countless examples of "education as therapy," a practice of "changing the child's values by techniques such as attitude questionnaires which dig into the privacy of the child and his family, psychological games in the classroom, and forcing the child to make adult decisions about such matters as suicide and murder, marriage and divorce, abortion and adoption."[7] An examination of the books found in many public school libraries and media centers will reveal titles that many Christian parents will find objectionable. One elementary school parent I spoke with was dismayed to find that an entire section of her child's reading book was devoted to poetry and prose about witches and goblins, complete with full color illustrations. A conference with the principal produced an alternative assignment, but many parents have neither the time to read nor the access to every textbook their student uses in school.

As educators, you probably have more to do with the character of the next generation than anyone else. In a sense you are the architects of that generation. Greed is the order of the day in a society preoccupied at all levels with the pursuit of bottom-lines, a society which celebrates consumption, careerism, and winning, and lives by the creed of "I've-got-mine-Jack." You must fling open the doors and find new ways of learning more about each other's values and spiritual traditions and what we all hold in common.
Television producer **NORMAN LEAR** at the National Education Association Convention, Kansas City, 1990

The selection standards used by public school teachers and librarians will not be the same standards used in the home- or Christian school library. Home schoolers cite many unfavorable educational practices, some of which can be found in the very best of public schools: "intense competition in every aspect of school life; rigid schedules that don't leave time for kids to pursue their own interests; insistence on conformity that drains initiative; the practice of grouping children according to their test scores; and failure to teach children how to think for themselves."[8]

Tenure and unions

The grip that tenure laws and unions hold on many school systems, particularly those in large cities, has caused many, both Christians and non-Christians, to give up on public schools. Tenure laws frequently tie administrators' hands with regard to incompetent teachers, and iron-clad negotiated contracts have reduced many systems to a battleground rather than a place of learning.

Public school quality and/or academic climate is often tied to location and real estate values

——————◆——————

Great disparities exist in the education and schooling offered to children from various communities that are reflective of differences in race, ethnicity, and social class. These glaring disparities not only represent economic inequities but also differences in political realities, cultural idioms, and ethnic histories.

SARA LAWRENCE LIGHTFOOT, *Worlds Apart: Relationships Between Families and Schools*

Unfortunately, the funding structure of public education, which relies on local property tax, results in great disparity between the public schools in rich and poor communities. This difference can go well beyond the obvious criteria of more books, better programs, and more well-qualified teachers. The culture and climate of the schools may be vastly different as well. Studies of public schools have shown that lower-class and minority schools and curricula tend to emphasize conformity to external rules and exhibit a high degree of discipline. This kind of training prepares students for jobs and roles in life where they will be the "supervised," not necessarily the "supervisor." The emphasis of upper-middle-class schools and curricula is on the internalization of values and self-direction over the conformity to rules. Students may engage in more study groups, individualized projects, and flexible scheduling.[9] Parents who desire the characteristics of the upper-middle-class school, but do not have the resources to live in that area, may find that home- and Christian school alternatives are more acceptable.

In the past five years, no statistically significant differences have appeared in either the grades people give their local schools or the public schools nationally. 43% of the respondents gave their local public schools A's and B's while only 24% gave those same grades to the public schools nationally. 57% of the parents who have students in public schools gave their schools A's and B's. The poorest grades for local schools came from residents of large cities and nonwhites. STANLEY M. ELAM and ALEC M. GALLUP, "21st Annual Gallup Poll of the Public's Attitudes Toward the Public Schools" in *Phi Delta Kappan*

What You Need to Know to Be a Successful Public School Parent

If you're well on your way to choosing the public school option, here are some helpful hints to make your experience a successful one.

Do your part at home
No matter where your child is being schooled, you have a number of important responsibilities at home. But these responsibilities are doubly important if your child is enrolled in the public school. You must continually reinforce the values and expectations of your own family with regard to behavior of all kinds—language, music, movies, books, clothing, and discipline.

Your children will be exposed to many different subcultures and lifestyles when they attend the public school. You must constantly set forth and explain what makes your family different and why. You must do this, however, in the context of supporting the public school.

If you reach the point where you are criticizing the textbooks, finding fault with the teacher, and undermining the administration at every turn, your child will have a difficult time doing well. On the other hand, your child needs to realize that just because "the teacher said so" doesn't make it truth.

The responsibility for staying "tuned-in" is a major one for the public school parent. You must find a comfortable zone between "hyper-reactivity" and "total unawareness." Many parents find this role an uncomfortable one because of its ambiguity and uncertainty.

Be a supportive parent

Supportive parents don't necessarily like everything either their child or the school does, but they have developed communication skills that enable them to talk about problems and arrive at solutions. Supportive parents listen to both sides of an issue before reaching a conclusion. They offer support to both the child and the school, realizing that always protecting the child to preserve their fragile parental ego or never holding the school accountable to avoid confrontation will accomplish nothing.

Get involved

Join the PTA, volunteer in the classroom or library, or even run for the school board. Involvement provides you with information about what is happening, influence over decisions that are made, and an inside track for achieving the goals you have for your child.

Communicate

Attend school board meetings and express your opinions on relevant issues. Talk to the school principal about what your expectations are for your child and the school. Meet with your child's teacher often—both formally and informally. Getting to know that teacher well will insure that your concerns will be addressed.

◆

We in public education can do much more to respond to the concerns of evangelicals, as we have learned to respond to other groups raising legitimate concerns about the schools.

Much depends upon how you approach us. If you begin by condemning us, by attributing to us a determination to brainwash your children in secular humanism, we will respond defensively and shut you out. If you ask for the opportunity to work with us to assure that your concerns for your children—concerns which we share, for they are in a sense "our children" as well—are met, we will respond gladly, or many of us will.

CHARLES L. GLENN, "What Evangelicals Should Expect of Public Schools" in *The Reformed Journal*

Be reasonable

Don't overreact. The public schools aren't always brainwashing your children. There isn't a secular humanist around every corner. You must realize that the public schools will not promote religious practices in the classroom. To expect them to do otherwise is unreasonable.

Have high expectations

You have every reason to expect that the public schools will offer an educational program that meets the needs of your child. You should expect high academic standards, good discipline, superior teaching, and strong administrative leadership. When you don't find these things, demand them. There are many ways to bring the change about.

Use established channels to effect change

While you and your child may not be able to wait for positive change to occur in his or her classroom, parents do have the power to remove ineffective teachers and administrators. They do have the power to raise expectations for discipline and academic standards, and they can accomplish these tasks in a spirit of cooperation and improvement. When you do have a concern, handle it in private and follow the chain of command. School board member Kathleen Cruse points out the importance of making your appeal in a reasonable and positive way. She recommends that if you really want change, "don't fight your battles in the newspaper. Once it's in the newspaper, it's too late for the change to be positive."

I like America's schools. I like them because I like living in America, and I am just naive enough to believe that schools have something to do with the quality of life in the society they serve. I see the need for some improvement. But I do not believe a major overhaul is necessary.

In addition to schools, I am excited about American students. As I travel to schools throughout the country, I am impressed with students individually and collectively. Certainly there are problem cases. But the vast majority of the students I see are cheerful, industrious young people who are working hard to develop themselves and their talents.

CLIFF SCHIMMELS in *The Blackboard Fumble*

Resources to Help You Be a More Informed Public School Parent

The following books, organizations, and free and inexpensive materials will help you become a more knowledgeable and effective public school parent.

Books

❑ Cutright, Melitta
The National PTA Talks to Parents: How to Get the Best Education for Your Child
Doubleday, 1989
Up-to-date suggestions from the parent organization of the public schools. Some local public schools disagree with the political involvement and demand for funds of this national organization and establish parent groups that are independent.

❑ Frith, Terry
Secrets Parents Should Know About the Public Schools
Simon & Schuster, 1986

A former public school administrator shares "secrets" about the system that are usually reserved for those on the inside.

☐ Harrison, Charles
Public Schools USA
Williamson Publishing, 1988
Evaluates the quality of hundreds of public schools, mostly in metropolitan areas.

☐ House, H. Wayne, editor
Schooling Choices: An Examination of Private, Public, and Home Education
Multnomah Press, 1988
Three authors make a case for the schooling option they believe is the "right" one. Also included is a critique of each of the positions by the other contributors. The participants become a bit defensive about their own turf, but the arguments offer food for thought.

☐ Laughy, Linwood
The Interactive Parent: How to Help Your Child Survive and Succeed in the Public Schools
Mountain Meadow Press, 1988
This volume has some outstanding resources, among them an excellent glossary, a seven-step problem solving process, and a classroom observation guide.

☐ Nemko, Marty and Barbara
How to Get a Private School Education in a Public School

Acropolis Books Ltd., 1986
A wonderful book that gives you dozens of ideas on how to get the most out of the public school. I can tell you from experience that the ideas work. I've used most of them as a parent. The Nemkos have provided a multitude of outstanding suggestions for making any educational experience better. This is a book I wish I'd written.

☐ Oakes, Jeannie and Martin Lipton
Making the Best of Schools
Yale University Press, 1990
A well-written and thoughtful book. The chapter on tracking (placing children in learning groups based on their ability) contains information you won't find anywhere else. Oakes is also the author of *Keeping Track: How Schools Structure Inequality* (Yale University Press, 1985).

☐ Rioux, William
You Can Improve Your Child's School
Simon & Schuster, 1980
Ideas for working with your local school to effect change.

☐ Schimmels, Cliff
How to Shape Your Child's Education
David C. Cook Publishing, 1989
Previously published as *How to Help Your Child Thrive and Survive in the Public Schools*
Advice from an experienced Christian educator on how to make the public schools work for your family.

❑ Schimmels, Cliff
Notes from the World's Oldest Freshman
David C. Cook Publishing, 1989
Previously published as *I Was a High School Drop-In*
If you want to get a taste of the contemporary public high school, follow Cliff as he enrolls as the world's oldest freshman.

❑ Sidey, Ken, editor
The Blackboard Fumble
Victor Books, 1989
A variety of outstanding educators examine the need for the public schools to uphold and foster basic moral standards. If you're planning to send your children to public school, this book is a "must" for you.

❑ Towns, Elmer L.
Have the Public Schools Had It?
Thomas Nelson, 1974
Although a bit dated, this volume contains some excellent information to help you bring about positive change in your public school.

Organizations

The following organizations provide information about public schooling, as well as support for parents who are attempting to change and improve the public schools. Write to them for further information. Where indicated, booklets and brochures are available.

☐ Council for Basic Education
725 Fifteenth St. NW
Washington, D.C. 20005
202-347-4171
Fax 202-347-5047
The Council for Basic Education is a nonprofit organization that "advocates schooling in the liberal
arts for all students and speaks as an independent
critical voice on school reform." Two publications,
Basic Education, a monthly that provides comment
and criticism on educational issues, and *Perspective,*
a quarterly that provides in-depth analysis and comment, are available by subscription.

☐ Institute for Responsive Education
605 Commonwealth Ave.
Boston, MA 02215
617-353-3309
The Institute for Responsive Education (IRE) is a
nonprofit public interest organization that promotes
parent and citizen involvement in education with a
special emphasis on equity issues. They publish
numerous reports and encourage citizen involvement
in school improvement.

☐ Lawyers' Christian Fellowship
3931 E. Main St.
Columbus, OH 43209

☐ National Committee for Citizens in Education
410 Wilde Lake Village Green

73

Columbia, MD 21044
301-997-9300

❐ SchoolMatch
800-992-5323
Provides a computerized service that relies on statistics such as school size, pupil-to-teacher ratios, teachers' salaries, and test scores to match students with public or private schools. The service costs $97.50.

6

Christian Schools:
God's Mandate for Christians?

Some of our friends object to the "hothouse"
environment of a Christian day school . . . there may be
a perfectly valid place for a hothouse, both for plants and
for children. Surely nourishment and training in a hothouse
will make for a stronger plant when it is later transplanted
and is forced to stand up to the elements.
JOE BAYLY in *The Basis for a Christian School*

*E*ven though one of the best public schools in Wheaton, Illinois is right down the street from where they live, Patrick and Mary Kay Brooke send their daughter, Emily, age 8, to Wheaton Christian Grammar School. "We made the choice before she was born," says Mary Kay, "and started saving money for the tuition right away."

For the Brooke family, the decision was an easy one. Although they both attended public schools and large secular universities, Christian education is a major part of their lives today. Mary Kay teaches preschool three days per week at the Wheaton Bible Church, where Jeffrey, age 5, is in prekindergarten. Patrick is Controller of Accounts at Wheaton College. They believe they have a responsibility to take advantage of their young children's abilities to absorb Bible stories and memory verses, and they want as much Christian teaching as possible for them during the early years.

As a former teacher in both Christian and public schools, Mary Kay is aware of the differences between the two. She knows it is impossible for teachers and students to pray together in public school classrooms. And she knows that the curriculum in the public school cannot be centered in God's truth.

"I think that academic excellence and the nurturing of good work habits are also important, and private schools can often do a better job of this," Mary Kay adds. But she laughs when asked about whether or not her daughter will be sheltered from the real world in a totally Christian environment.

"The big playhouse in our back yard is a beehive of neighborhood activity," she explains. "We always have birthday parties for both school and neighborhood friends. In fact, we've even been dropping a nearby neighborhood child off at the public school on our way to Christian Grammar when needed."

As the only family in the neighborhood whose children do not attend the public school, Patrick and Mary Kay demonstrate an obvious sense of mission to minister to their neighbors. Only recently did Emily wonder about the difference between her school and that of her friends. Mary Kay and Patrick explained that the difference is God.

"Public schools can teach children science," Patrick says, "but they can't teach them about the Creator behind the science. At home we can teach our children God's Word, but at school the truth can be integrated into all of the academic areas."

Christian schools are on the move. Their enrollments are growing each year as more parents decide that the other options just don't measure up. Lyle and Kathleen Morrow, both suburban public school teachers, have chosen the Christian school option for their children. They transferred their son to a non-denominational Christian school in sixth grade when they realized that both his academic and social development were being adversely affected by an undesirable peer group. They are sorry they didn't make the move sooner, and point to the following advantages of Christian schooling.

Advantages of Christian Schooling

Friends/peer group with clear-cut moral values, academic talent, and the motivation to do well in school

As parents, we frequently don't realize how important the social aspects of school are in a child's life. Most children will rate their friends as a more important influence on them than even their teachers. While not every student enrolled in a Christian school is necessarily a Christian or a gifted student, the peer group in this environment is far less likely to introduce your child to drugs, sex, obscene language, and alcohol than in a public school setting and far more likely to provide good role models and influences with regard to studies and academic achievement. A Christian high-school student put it this way: "Kids either change when they come here or don't stay very long."

◆

Unlike public school youth, they (Christian school students) endure little or none of the ambiguity and tension that can develop when teachers, peers, parents, and neighbors reinforce different values. Though they will live in a society replete with competing alternatives, (Christian school) provides them with a clear-cut identity.
ALAN PESHKIN, *God's Choice: The Total World of a Fundamentalist Christian School*

Christian focus
While the public school must by necessity of its mission be pluralistic in focus, the Christian school can be single-minded in its goals and purpose—"to glorify God." The mission is always clearly stated for teachers, parents, and students, and all of the school's activities and programs are developed with the Christian world view in mind.

Biblical instruction as an academic subject, and other subjects taught with a biblical perspective
While it is estimated that only ten to fifteen percent of parents choose the Christian school option for religious

reasons,[1] the parents and Christian school staff members I interviewed almost always mentioned it as one of the most important advantages of a Christian school education. The integration of faith and learning that serves as the foundation for the Christian school philosophy provides students with "education for righteousness, education for morality, education for truth, and education for life."[2]

Christian staff

Caring Christian teachers can interact with students in ways that even the most dedicated Christian public school teacher will never be able to. Through role modeling, prayer, and consistent integration of curriculum with biblical principles, the Christian teacher can have an enormous impact on the life of a student. The Christian school staff, while certainly not as well paid as their public school counterparts, often work longer hours, are more involved in their students' home and school lives, and develop their own curriculum materials to meet the challenge of integrating faith and learning.

Competition in athletics and academics that takes place within a biblical framework

The competitive, win-at-any-cost philosophy that pervades the world at large is moderated and mediated in the Christian school environment. Competition is placed in a biblical framework and students learn to appreciate and value individuals based on who they are and not on what they achieve.

Textbooks, library books, and curriculum that reflect the Christian world view

Christian educators are vigorous in their condemnation of secular textbooks. And their criticisms are often well justified. They find them to be filled with teachings that condone humanism, socialism, situation ethics, relativism, and anti-God and anti-biblical philosophies.[3] Parents who have transferred their children to public schools from the Christian schools concur. While Christian school parents still have a responsiblity to be aware of what their children are reading and learning at school, they can be assured that whatever is taught will be within the Christian context. While students may read about evolution, communism, existentialism, and humanism, their readings will be done from a Christian perspective and discussed with Christian teachers.

◆

The Coleman Report, a federally funded research project found the following:

1. Private schools provide better character and personality development than public schools.

2. Private schools provide a safer, more disciplined, and more ordered environment than public schools.

3. Private schools are more successful in creating an interest in learning than public schools.

4. Private schools encourage interest in higher education and lead more of their students to attend college than public schools with comparable students.

5. Private schools are more efficient than public schools, accomplishing their educational task at lower cost.

6. Private schools have smaller class sizes, and thus allow teachers and students to have greater contact.
Public and Private Schools, National Center for Education Statistics

---

Christian School Disadvantages

While the vigorous supporters of Christian education usually emphasize only the positive aspects of this option, parents whose children are long-time attenders of Christian schools point out the following possible problem areas.

Quality of staff
Grace Jordan, a successful professional and single parent, believes that staff quality is a significant problem in some Christian schools. Her two daughters have attended Christian schools exclusively, but not without some difficulties along the way. Grace points out that Christian schools often exhibit major weaknesses where children with learning problems are concerned. She says that Christian school teachers are sometimes limited in methodology, not always sensing a need to seek alternate means of teaching when a child is not learning well.

Dottie and Mark Williams's experience also focused on an unresponsive teacher. They felt that since teachers generally are paid less in Christian schools, they may be more limited in their educational background. Grace Jordan was outspoken in her commentary: "Competent teachers are the exception rather than the rule. Christians sometimes find it difficult to deal with 'you're not good enough' when determining a teacher's skill as an educator. Being a Christian seems to be the sole criteria." In some schools teachers are paid far less than their public school counterparts and are asked to sign pledges relating to their behavior outside of school. This practice can severely limit the pool from which to draw competent, growing educators.

Fewer special programs and/or course offerings
Christian schools cannot always offer the range of programs and services that are available in public schools. Libraries, art, music, physical education, and computers are a few of the services that may not be found in every Christian school. At the high-school level, fewer courses may be offered than in a large, comprehensive public high school. One parent noted that faculty at the Christian high school her children attend frequently double up and teach courses for which they have little preparation or training.

High cost

◆

Those who are not attracted by the isolation of home education and who cannot win the zero-sum game of public-school orthodoxy may seek out private schooling. As with home education, some extra financial or emotional resources are required, and it is rarely the impoverished, the victims of discrimination, or the overworked who can afford private schools.

STEPHEN ARONS, *Compelling Belief: The Culture of American Schooling*

The high cost of a Christian school education can often create a financial burden for low- and middle-income families, if not eliminate that option from their consideration altogether. Economic discrimination against the less affluent members of society that keeps them from participating in Christian education further insulates the wealthier students who attend. In some cases, low-income students who do receive scholarships to attend the Christian school may still be alienated socially and culturally from their wealthier counterparts by the creation of a "caste system."

Fewer channels for solving problems
While Christian parents have a certain amount of power because they pay the tuition bills and can choose to remove their children from the school at any time, it is often difficult for parents to question the authority and policies of the school. One parent I interviewed called it the "we are ordained of God" syndrome. When parents question a methodology or decision made in the classroom, the teacher and administrator can and do invoke "God's will." Solving problems collaboratively can be difficult if this attitude prevails. Parents who are not major contributors or part of the governing board are

often disenfranchised from local Christian school decision making.

Parental involvement and additional financial support is often mandated

In addition to paying the tuition, parents of Christian school students are often expected, and in some cases mandated, to make additional financial contributions, participate in fund-raising activities, and volunteer in classrooms and/or the supervision of extra-curricular activities. While the parents I interviewed found these activities to be worthwhile, they wished for more choice and flexibility.

Highly sheltered environment

The highly sheltered environment is seen by many Christian parents to be exactly what they are looking for. There will be few, if any, opportunities for their children to be corrupted. But there are some Christian parents who find this environment to be too rigid and controlled. Some students, they feel, are just waiting for the opportunity to "break out and cut loose." One parent I interviewed felt that Christian school kids can sometimes "burn out" on Sunday school and church. The students feel they know so much, they don't want to hear the same material and application over and over again.

Another parent who had made the public school choice after being in the Christian school for a number of years said she didn't want her child to become a "Christian clone." A youth director with whom I spoke lamented the fact that the students in his youth group who attended a local Christian high school weren't as involved in the outreach programs as the public high-school students. "The Christian high-school kids are so self-contained and isolated," he said. "They have the 'we are the church' mentality."

---◆---

What makes the Christian school movement so utterly mind-boggling is that it has begun to seriously undercut a century-long (humanistic) trend in popular education in America.

In practice, this means that over a million school children in America today are receiving a completely different interpretation of the basis of knowledge, truth and reality than their counterparts in public schools.

JEREMY RIFKIN and TED HOWARD, *The Emerging Order: God in an Age of Scarcity*

Mixed messages

Attending school with Christian young people can often be misleading, as one mother pointed out. "You don't always know if someone is really a committed Christian. In a secular setting, kids have to be more definitive about their faith. Here (at the Christian school) kids can masquerade as Christians if they go through the motions." Another parent pointed out the confusion her daughter faced when finding out that one of her Christian high-school friends had just had an abortion.

"Siege" mentality

Research into some of the Christian school literature reveals the "siege" mentality that is noted by Leslie Tarr.[4] Christian school proponents frequently exhibit one or more of the following characteristics as described by Tarr: identifying a Christian world view with condemnation of passing fads such as hair or clothing styles and popular music; equation of right-wing politics with an approved Christian political stance; a condemnation of the sins of the flesh and little rebuke of the sins of the spirit; little capacity for self-criticism, and an exclusiveness based on the above tenets. While these characteristics are certainly not typical of the vast majority of Christian schools, parents I interviewed frequently mentioned them as disadvantages.

What You Need to Know to Be a Successful Christian School Parent

Roy W. Lowrie, Jr., a noted Christian educator, offers the following warnings for parents who have decided to enroll their children in a Christian school.[5]

Christian school teachers don't replace the training in the home by parents

Many Christian parents become complacent about their own personal teaching and training responsiblities once they have their child safely enrolled in the local Christian school. No matter how excellent the

Christian school is, our responsibilities as parents still continue.

More and more families are choosing private education because of their dissatisfaction with the public schools. And many parents are turning to Protestant evangelical schools for the moral and religious grounding they want their children to have.

While there are no figures available on total enrollment in these schools, the Association of Christian Schools International, the largest of the Protestant evangelical educational groups, reports that the number of students in its affiliated schools grew from 186,000 in 1978 to 390,000 in 1984.

GENE I. MAEROFF, "Private School Enrollment Takes Off" in *The New York Times*

Christian schools can't resolve all of the problems that have developed in the home

Parents sometimes feel that because they are paying tuition and because the school is Christian, teachers and administrators will be able to solve severe learning and discipline problems—indeed work educational miracles and do it in a short period of time. Such is not the case. The educational expertise of even the most outstanding Christian teacher can't remediate a child who's two years below grade level in the first two months of school. Nor can they give a slow learner twenty more IQ points.

***While Christian teachers will care about your
child's academic and behavioral problems, they
will not excuse or overlook them***
Parents are sometimes led to believe that the caring,
Christian teacher has an obligation to be more tolerant
and accepting of behavioral and academic problems—
giving students favorable grades or moving them ahead
even though they have not learned their lessons. Christian love does not include pretending that severe student
problems do not exist.

***Every student in your child's class won't be a
wholesome person who will be a positive influence on your child***
While the composition of the student body was cited as
one of the prime advantages of the Christian school, you
must be aware that not all parents who send their
children to the Christian school believe as you do. Dr.
David Roth, headmaster of a Christian high school,
summed it up this way: "We're not an angel factory. We
can't build fences high enough to keep out the Adamic
nature. We can mitigate the worldly influences, but we
can't sanitize the kids." Some parents have specifically
chosen the Christian school option to "straighten up" a
child who is in academic or behavioral trouble. So don't
be surprised if your child picks up some bad habits at
school, even at the Christian school.

Christian schools aren't perfect
The proponents of Christian schools argue their cases so
eloquently that parents sometimes expect "heaven"

when they arrive for the first day of class. But Christian schools have problems—problem teachers, problem parents, and problem students. Realistic Christian school parents don't let these imperfections stand in the way of a positive school experience for their children. They support the school and its teachers.

◆

Shattering Myths about Christian School Education

Myth: It is un-American to send your children to a Christian school.

Reality: Bible-centered Protestant Christian schools existed in America 217 years before public schools were established.

Myth: Christian schools are "white-flight" academies.

Reality: James Coleman reported in 1981 that minorities who attend private and religious schools are "substantially less segregated in the private sector than in the public sector."

Myth: Christian schools cannot compete economically with the public schools. Therefore, their academic program suffers.

Reality: Nationwide testing of 240,000 students by the Association of Christian Schools International shows the average achievement level to be one year and six months ahead of the national norm.

Myth: Only wealthy families send their children to Christian schools.

Reality: The Council for American Private Education reported in 1986 that "as a group, the parents of private

school children belie the image of an affluent elite. Sixty percent earn less than $20,000 a year."
PAUL A. KIENEL, *About Christian School Education*

How Can You Help?

In addition to Lowrie's specific hints for Christian school parents, the tips included in Chapter Five for public school parents will also help your Christian schooling experience be a positive one. Just because you're sending your child to a Christian school doesn't mean you can relax and put parenting on automatic pilot. Christian school teachers and administrators are quick to point out that involved parents always make a child's education more meaningful.

Do your part at home. James Coleman's study cited earlier in the chapter pointed out the benefits of having your child enrolled in a private (Christian) school. These results come from having committed and involved parents who are supporting the school, backing the teacher, and holding their kids accountable for their homework.

Be a supportive parent
Many Christian parents have unreasonable expectations about what the school can be and do. They are quick to find fault and lay blame on the school. The same advice I gave to public school parents applies here: Listen to both sides of an issue before making a decision or reaching a conclusion. Try to support both the school and your child.

Get involved
Volunteer whenever you can. Your children's knowledge that you are in the school building or working on a school project will give them an extra boost of self-confidence and will give you an understanding of the school environment.

◆

My observations suggest that Christian schools may make as great a difference in the lives of parents, teachers, and religious leaders as in the lives of their students.
SUSAN ROSE, *Keeping Them Out of the Hands of Satan: Evangelical Schooling in America*

Communicate
Attend all the meetings you can. Talk to the principal about what your expectations are for your child and the school. Meet with your child's teacher often—both formally and informally. We always had our teachers over for a Christmas tea. Each year as they moved through school we included more teachers and the group got a little larger. This informal gathering was a way for my children to interract with their teachers on a different level and the teachers had an opportunity to be in our home and know us as a family.

Use established channels to effect change
When you have a concern about something that is happening at school, handle it in private and follow the chain

of command. Always start with the classroom teacher and then move to administrator and finally board members. Once your grievance or problem becomes public, reconciliation and solution are far more difficult.

Roy W. Lowrie, Jr. holds the highest standards for Christian school parents. He believes that even a Christian school is less effective when the following conditions are not present in your home. The statements in italics are mine, added to encourage single-parent readers. I believe that the presence of only one parent in a family, for whatever the reason, does not preclude the establishment of an effective Christian home.

- Christ is the head of the home.

- A loving, kind, just, father *(or mother)* is the head of the family.

- The family shares a devotional experience in the home each day.

- The parents *(parent)* put the Bible into practice in their lives.

- The children see their parents *(parent)* depending upon the Lord for everything.

- The father and *(or)* mother have control of their children with dignity.

- The parents *(parent)* carefully supervise the close friendships developed by their children.

- The family is characterized by strong bonds of love, unity, and togetherness.

- The children can talk freely with their parents *(parent)* about problems.

- The standards and rules for the children are fair, clear, and are enforced consistently.

- The mother and *(or)* father show affection for each other and for their children.[6]

◆

Someone asked me recently, "How can we help change the public school system?" My response was as follows: "Any public school system exists to accommodate the people it serves. As a result of this, virtually all religion of any kind has been removed from our schools, along with the original concept of the American or Canadian philosophy of life."

For Christians to have an impact on our society, we need to develop a generation of young people who think biblically, who look at life from God's eye and who put biblical principles into practice. We will then, as a body, truly become the salt and the light that God intended us to be, impacting greatly on our society. Producing this kind of society can be accomplished only as we train young people from birth to

adulthood from God's perspective. One of the major contributions to the process, augmenting the home and extend-
ing the Church, is the Christian school.
PAUL B. SMITH, foreword to *Sowing for Excellence: Educating God's Way*

Resources to Help You Be a More Informed Christian School Parent

The following books, organizations, and free and inexpensive materials will help you become a more knowledgeable and effective Christian school parent.

Books

The following list is by no means a complete one. Many
others can be obtained by writing to the organizations
found in the resource list.

❏ Cummings, David B., editor
The Basis for a Christian School
Presbyterian and Reformed Publishing Co., 1982
The Christian Education Association cooperated with
the outstanding contributors to this volume, among
them Mark Noll and the late Joseph Bayly. Note
especially the fine chapter on the God-given parent-
child relationship by the editor.

❏ Gaebelein, Frank E.
The Pattern of God's Truth
Moody Press, 1968

Originally published by Oxford University Press, this
volume is scholarly and thoughtful. Gaebelein presents a powerful case for the integration of faith and
learning.

☐ House, H. Wayne, editor
Schooling Choices
Multnomah Press, 1988
Kenneth Gagnel, professor and chair of the depart-
ment of Christian education at Dallas Theological
Seminary, is the author of the section on Christian
schooling.

☐ Peshkin, Alan
*God's Choice: The Total World of a Fundamentalist
Christian School*
University of Chicago Press, 1986
Although the author is clearly not a Christian, his
ethnographic study of Bethany Baptist Academy,
pseudonym for a Christian school in a Chicago suburb,
is an accurate and impartial portrayal of institutional
life in a Christian school.

☐ Rose, Susan
*Keeping Them Out of the Hands of Satan: Evangelical
Schooling in America*
Routledge, Chapman and Hall, Inc., 1988
Another fine ethnographic study of two Christian
schools in upstate New York, one an independent,
charismatic covenant community and the other a
predominantly working-class fundamentalist Baptist
school.

❏ Schindler, Claude E., Jr. and Pacheco Pyle
Educating for Eternity
Tyndale House Publishers, Inc., 1979
This small volume provides a rationale for Christian education. The authors also give suggestions for "starting up" a Christian school.

Organizations

The following organizations provide information about Christian schooling and give support to parents who are attempting to establish their own Christian school. Write to them for further information. Where indicated, booklets and brochures are also available.

❏ American Association of Christian Schools
6601 N.W. 167th Street
Hialea (Miami), FL 33015

❏ Association of Christian Schools International
P.O. Box 4097
Whittier, CA 90607
213-694-4791
Fax 213-690-6234
This is the largest of the Christian school associations and its services and publications are impressive. ACSI is "dedicated to fostering unity among all Christian schools and educators, edifying, exhorting and encouraging God's people through Christian education." They publish an extensive list of materials—curricula, books for parents, teachers, students, and Christian school board members. *The ACSI Advocate*

is a slick newspaper with world news and views that affect Christian education. A brochure and order blank are available by calling or writing.

❏ Christian Schools Today
464 Malin Rd.
Newtown Square, PA 19073
215-356-5639
Write for the brochure "Marks of a Strong Christian Home."

❏ National Christian Education Association
Box 28
Wheaton, IL 60189
An arm of the National Association of Evangelicals, this organization's sole mission is the publication of a variety of inexpensive pamphlets and booklets including a "getting started" packet for those wanting to establish a Christian school.

❏ National Union of Christian Schools
865 Twenty-Eight Southeast
Grand Rapids, MI 49508
Christian Schools International (started in 1920 by the Dutch Calvinists, an association of Reformed Schools).

7

Home, Sweet Home:
Is It the Classroom for You?

It is the combination of liberation from the classroom and the public school curricula that makes the Christian home-school option superior to all other options in education.
GREGG HARRIS in *Schooling Choices: An Examination of Private, Public, & Home Education*

*O*n school days, when all her neighborhood friends are hurrying off to school, Stacy Armstrong, a seventh grader, is enjoying a two-mile hike with her mom. At the time when her friends are just beginning their school day, Stacy already has been working on math problems and science experiments. She and her mother are early risers, and their home-schooling experience is not bound by traditional schedules. They begin working at 6:15 a.m. Both Stacy and her brother Matthew have attended public schools, but their parents felt that much of one year was wasted academically. The Armstrongs opted for home-schooling their children at that point.

Anita, a former teacher, is highly organized and structured. She plans her lessons six weeks in advance and seeks out all of the resources she can to make learning exciting and enriching for her home-schoolers. She belongs to a local support group of over 65 families, which plans extracurricular activities and field trips. Her husband, a local minister, has a flexible schedule, which allows his wife to go to Bible study and pursue individual interests.

Anita is enthusiastic about the advantages of home schooling. "One of the primary benefits of home schooling is the positive reinforcement a mother is constantly able to give. There is no one calling my child a 'dummy' or laughing at a wrong answer. My children have acquired our family's morals rather than those of their peers."

Keeping School All in the Family

While her neighbors are rushing off to jobs, aerobics classes, or lunch with friends, Shawn Strannigan is teaching reading and math to Lindsay, 7, and Danielle, 5. Candyce, 3, plays quietly or watches "Sesame Street" while the Strannigan School is in session. While some mothers may give only lip service to the "quality time" concept, Shawn is guiding her children through a comprehensive basic curriculum.

A published author, Shawn is articulate about the decision she and her husband Greg have made to home-school their children.

"I'm not a militant home schooler," she emphatically states. "Home schooling is not for everyone, but I believe that God wants me to do this. I don't believe in withdrawing from the world. That's not the reason for our decision. I'm home-schooling to build my children up, not to shelter them from the world. I want them to be well prepared to face the world someday."

Just two years ago, Shawn was eagerly awaiting the day Lindsay would go off to kindergarten. She already had enrolled her in the local public school. But that summer she attended a home-schooling convention in Sacramento. The daughter of a prominent home-schooling spokesman, Raymond Moore, spoke to the convention attendees, and it was at that moment Shawn felt led to try it with her children. She says she has not been sorry. "Every year I love it more. The rewards have definitely outweighed the disadvantages."

Shawn and Greg are not critical of their public schools. But they realize their limitations. "At home we can put God in the history and science lessons, right where he belongs. We have the freedom to teach whatever we want to."

Shawn is not without support in her home-schooling endeavor. Enrolled in the home-extension program of the Freedom Christian School in Fair Oaks, California, she receives help with curriculum, lesson plans, and testing from the faculty and administration there. The school keeps attendance records and offers the legal accountability that often is needed to keep local school officials reassured.

In addition, Shawn participates in a "team home school," joining with other mothers to share skills and knowledge. To critics who question the lack of socialization opportunities for children schooled at home, the Strannigans point with pride to the group of neighborhood children who have come to check out the craft projects and science experiments completed by Lindsay and Danielle during their school day.

"Our home is the hub of the neighborhood," Shawn proudly points out. "The neighborhood kids want to be here because they often think that what we're doing is more interesting than what's happening at the local school."

Shawn feels that home schooling is a dual commitment, and she relies on her husband Greg, minister of the Sylvan Oaks Christian Church, for support and encouragement. He substitutes regularly to give her an occasional break from teaching. Since Greg has recently received his California high-school teaching credential, there may someday be two teachers in the Strannigan family—one at home and one in school.

Advantages of Home Schooling

◆

No schoolroom can match the simplicity and power of the home in providing three-dimensional, firsthand education. The school, not the home, is the substitute, and its highest function is to complement the family. The family is still the social base, and must be, if our society is to survive. Let's leave no stone unturned to guarantee the fullest freedom of the home and the rights of parents to determine the education of their children.

RAYMOND and DOROTHY MOORE, *Home-Grown Kids: A Practical Handbook for Teaching Your Children at Home*

Possible in any setting (mission field, isolated rural area, inner city, a suburb)

Home schooling has been going on since the beginning of time. Only as we have become more "civilized" and "scientific" have we begun to believe that "professionals" can do a better job than parents. Many contemporary missionary families are beginning to feel that home school is far superior to boarding school. Greg Harris reports that home schooling is a growing option among Wycliffe missionaries. Cora Lee and Arno Enns, missionaries for many years in Argentina, would agree. They home-schooled their four daughters in conjunction with their attendance in national schools in Argentina for over a decade. Their bilingual education program prepared all four children for successful careers.

David and Donna Brown (mentioned in Chapter Five) combined the home-schooling option with Japanese school for their children. But the far-flung mission field is not the only convenient location for home schooling. The Colfax family, well-known home schoolers whose sons have all enrolled at Harvard, live on a goat farm in California. But you don't need to live in a remote location for home schooling to make sense. There are hundreds of home schoolers in suburbs and cities as well. It is the only schooling option that is not bound by the physical location of a building or the purchase of a home in a certain locale.

Parental involvement and complete control of a child's education
Home schooling gives parents the freedom to educate according to their personal convictions, using materials that make sense to them, and employing methodologies that work with their children. While some parents home-school for educational reasons, others do so for moral and religious reasons. They object to textbooks and cur-riculum that undermine the values and beliefs of the home. They want to have daily devotions with their children, spend time in Scripture memory work, and participate in community ministries together.

Sometimes a better setting in which "late bloomers" and children with problems can flourish
Many children just need time to "mature" or "outgrow" a problem. Mark and Sandy Coffman's son, Justin, was just such a youngster. A hearing problem during his preschool years delayed Mark's speech and language development. In a regular school setting he might have been placed in special education or diagnosed with a learning problem. At home, under the careful tutelage of his mother and father, he caught up beautifully. He needed time and individual attention—commodities in short supply in formal school settings. Justin will join

his older brother at Christian school next year with none of the baggage of "failure" that often accompanies a poor start in school.

◆

(T)he family is man's first and basic school. Parents have very extensively educated their child before the child ever sets foot inside a school. Moreover, every mother regularly performs the most difficult of all educational tasks, one which no school performs. The mother takes a small child, incapable of speaking or understanding a word in any language, and, in a very short time, teaches it the mother tongue. This is a difficult and painstaking task, but it comes simply and naturally in the family as an expression of the mother's love and the child's response to that love. At every stage of the child's life, the educational function of the home is the basic educational power in the life of the child.
ROUSAS J. RUSHDOONY, *Law and Liberty*

Nancy Wallace, in her book *Better Than School,* describes the troubles her son Ishmael had in first grade before she began to home-school him. He already knew how to read (he'd learned on his own) so the teacher gave him a third-grade workbook. Poor Ishmael didn't know anything about prepositions or suffixes and prefixes. The workbook exercises had nothing to do with knowing how to read. So even though he could read beautifully, he was frustrated and miserable, feeling he had failed.[1] Psychologist David Elkind[2] and home-school expert Raymond Moore[3] cite reams of research to support waiting until even the age of eight or ten to begin formal schooling.

Dena Wiesner is just such a parent. When her daughter was diagnosed with a visual problem, the doctor warned Dena that her daughter might be a late reader. In response, Dena has taken a low-key approach to reading, following Moore's cue, and now is seeing her patience begin to pay off.

Close family relationships
Home-schooled children learn to live with and love their siblings. They help each other with lessons and work on projects together. Moms of home-schooled students report that close bonds develop between brothers and sisters of different ages and interests, a rarity in many families where children spend more time with their age-mates from school than their families.

Peer group essentially controlled by parents
Parents who are concerned about the negative effects of peer pressure and the influence of a community without values can guide their child in the selection of friends and acquaintances.

◆

Psychologist Mona Maarse Delahooke compared fairly equivalent groups of 32 private school and 28 home-school children of about nine years of age. She found no significant difference between the two groups in reading, arithmetic, or intelligence scores. Likewise, both groups scored in the "well adjusted" range of the Roberts Apperception Test for Children.

One difference, however, did surface in Delahooke's study. Home-educated children appeared to be less peer oriented than those in schools. This finding tends to confirm that home-schooling may accomplish one additional purpose many Christian parents want it to: reduce the influence of peer pressure.

BRIAN RAY, "The Kitchen Classroom: Is Home Schooling Making the Grade?" in *Christianity Today*

A setting more like the real world

Home schoolers are quick to point out that the formal school setting is nothing like the "real world." Once children leave school, they rarely spend time exclusively with people their own age. They work and socialize with a variety of different age groups. Home schoolers whose parents structure the opportunities can be as comfortable helping with a brand-new baby as they can helping out at a local nursing home.

Quantity time

Today the phrase "quality time" is much overworked by parents who are looking for a way to explain their lack of involvement in their children's lives. There are many parents who do look upon twenty-four-hour-a-day, 365-day-a-year involvement with their children as more of a burden than a blessing. But for home-schooling parents, the opportunity to spend time getting to know their children as individuals is a prime advantage. Joylin Lane, a home schooler for eight years, cites this as one of the biggest reasons she made the home-school choice. "I don't want to look back at the years my children were in elementary school and wonder where the time went. I'll have lived with my kids since the day they were born." Joylin, whose oldest son, Matthew, entered the formal school setting for the first time as a sixth grader, is well aware of how much time formal schooling actually takes. "By the time Matthew comes home from school in the afternoon, he's too tired to do anything else."

◆

The typical home-school family is middle-class and white, and at least one of the parents has some college education. In something like nine out of ten such households the mother does most of the teaching. Boys and girls are equally likely to be taught at home.

ALFIE KOHN, "Home-Schooling" in *The Atlantic*

Little or no competition in the home setting
The minute a child enters the formal school setting, the comparisons begin. On the first day of school I've watched kindergarten parents eyeing other children to see how their child measures up. They want their child to be first—after all, that's the American way. Teachers prepare charts to keep track of how many books students have read, how far they can count, and how many soup labels they contributed to the PTA fund-raising drive.

There is competition on every hand. Students are measured, labeled, and sorted. While we all recognize that competition is part of an adult life, the young child who loses early and often in a highly competitive environment can have his self-esteem shattered. He may even give up.

Self-motivated rather than "lock-step" learning

◆

When Micki and David Colfax began teaching their four sons at home 15 years ago, they had no intention of sending them all to Harvard, but that's how it's turning out. Grant, 23, graduated from Harvard and has stayed on as a biology instructor; later this year he'll start a Fulbright scholarship in New Zealand. Drew, 20 is a premed sophomore. And last month Harvard mailed yet another acceptance letter to the Colfax goat farm in Boonville, Calif., for Reed, 17.

JEAN SELIGMANN with PAMELA ABRAMSON in *Newsweek*

While educators who work in institutionalized settings freely talk of "individualized learning" and "enrichment," the fact remains that the text or curriculum and the students in the class influence what is taught and how it is taught. Rarely, if ever, do students and teachers enjoy the luxury of spending an entire day on a single project or assignment. Rarely does the student have the freedom to pursue his or her own interests without regard for "curriculum" or "textbooks."

When my daughter Emily was eight she became fascinated with Egyptian history. Although I wasn't a formal home schooler, I would have qualified as an "underground" member. I encouraged her to pursue this interest. We checked books out of the library, bought more at the book store, visited museums, and purchased art supplies. Egypt consumed our lives for a period of time. At school, Emily would have been told that "we don't do Egypt until sixth grade." Recently, my daughter completed a university course on the same topic. "How was it?" I asked her.

"I learned most of what the professor was teaching when I was eight and nine," she answered.

It is true that we remember best what we are motivated to learn on our own. And learning in the home can travel down any path.

The Colfax family's curriculum was based on the homestead they built. The boys restored the land, planted gardens, and improved livestock—subjects not taught in any grade school I know. Their interest and expertise in the areas of biology, chemistry, and, subsequently, embryology and genetics grew out of their homestead project. Home schooling is perfect for the gifted student who is bored and irritated with the structure and rigidity of a system that prescribes when and how much learning each student will get. Children have time to pursue more special interests and hobbies since learning one-on-one is more efficient and more can be accomplished in a short time period. Home-schooled students frequently learn to use the community and its resources far more effectively than other children.

◆

Home-schooling is not for everybody, we believe. But it can be a desirable alternative in cases where peer influence is destructive, where inflexible schools are less able than the parents to meet the instructional needs of bright children, where the local school seems bent on teaching unbiblical values, where children with special needs cannot be properly accommodated by the schools, and where parental vision for education is potentially more broadening and less crushing than the standardized and routinized program available in local institutions.

DAVID NEFF, "Why Johnny Can't Stay Home" in *Christianity Today*

As idyllic as home schooling can sound when described by an enthusiastic practitioner, there are disadvantages that must be considered before making the choice.

Disadvantages of Home Schooling

Public pressure—either legal or just from friends, family, and neighbors

◆

When a family seeks approval of a home-education plan from a public authority, it is implicitly challenging the professionalization of education. . . .

Many educators seem to regard their occupational survival as dependent upon their insistence that they, and only they, can adequately define, create, and judge quality in education.
STEPHEN ARONS, *Compelling Belief: The Culture of American Schooling*

While home schooling is growing in popularity, there are still areas of the country where legal pressure can make life difficult for the home schooler. You can legally home-school in all states, but there is a wide variance regarding time and curriculum requirements and the degree to which local officials enforce, monitor, or even cooperate. The most pressure will likely come from family and friends who will question your motives, your ability to cope with the situation, and, in some cases, your sanity. As a home schooler, be prepared to spend a lot of time explaining and defending to other people what you do. An education official I spoke with who monitors home schoolers says his office frequently receives calls from neighbors of home schoolers. "They're complaining about kids playing outside in the middle of the day," he reports. His office is obligated to investigate complaints that are usually unfounded. "One parent teaching one child can accomplish more in three hours than one teacher teaching thirty kids in six hours," he adds. "It's not unreasonable that a home-schooled child will have a little more recess time. But most people just don't understand that." Some Christian friends may even criticize your decision, feeling that your children can best be schooled at the Christian school.

Lack of social contact with peers

While this is the most oft-mentioned disadvantage of home schooling, most parents I interviewed are aware of the problem and do an admirable job of compensating. Many belong to parent networks that provide social opportunities for children. CHOICE (Christian Home Oriented Individual Curriculum Experience), a group in suburban Chicago, offers field trips, gym (for a fee), swimming, cooking, and art classes. The group plans events around holidays and even puts on a Christmas program in a local auditorium. These events do not take place without much planning and organization on the part of committed individuals, however. Parents must pay for teachers and meeting places. As enriching as these various activities may be, they may not provide that "special friend" parents hope their children will have because of the limited number of children at any grade level. And your child may not have the opportunity to develop friendships on his or her own, away from the structure and watchful eye of Mom.

Sheltered, potentially over-protected environment

◆

Schools are environments that must support and encourage the child's movement away from the emotional and dependent constraints of family. Teachers build relationships that are qualitatively different from parent-child interactions; that are based on different criteria of evaluation and judgment. Their adult role is more neutralized and restrained as they apply generalized, universal expectations and visible rules.

SARA LAWRENCE LIGHTFOOT, *Worlds Apart: Relationships Between Families and Schools*

This is precisely the kind of environment that many home-schooling parents want for their children. But there are others who find the confinement of home unnecessarily restrictive. If your children will ultimately transfer to a conventional school setting, they need to be prepared for such traumatic events as showering in the locker room, playing team sports in the gym, and eating in the school lunch room.

Much time, organization, and commitment needed by parent

If you've mastered the skills of organization and time management, then this disadvantage will not bother you. "Home schooling takes a person who is extremely organized, if you want to do it justice," says Anita Armstrong. She laughs as she relates the slogan they have adopted at their home. "First we work, and then we play." If you want to do a good job, your work as a home-schooling parent will consume almost all of your time and energy.

Lack of objectivity about your child

We all think our children are perfect. And it's very difficult to be objective about them. One of the benefits of sending them out in the world is the opportunity they have to practice their social skills away from the watchful parental eye and get feedback that is honest and real about who they are and how they're doing. All children need a little fine-tuning and usually Mom and Dad don't have the objectivity to do that. The home-schooled child is so completely enmeshed with his mother that this fine-tuning may never take place.

Parental sacrifice

The total parental commitment that is needed to make home schooling work means that Mom (or somebody) will have to put most of her own personal life on hold. The home schoolers with whom I talked seem to have time for little else but home schooling. The movement is still too young to determine what effect this will have later on the emotional and psychological adjustment of the women involved, but care must be taken by the home teacher to develop a healthy personal life with friends and activities apart from home schooling.

The possibility of making faulty educational decisions, due to ignorance or misunderstanding

While avid home schoolers can get defensive if their credentials for teaching are questioned, in some cases they need to seek out the opinions of experts. One mom who has home-schooled her four children cited two examples where she feels her lack of educational expertise shortchanged her children. Converted to home schooling by Raymond Moore through reading his books and attending a workshop, she took very seriously his advice about delaying formal teaching. But she laments, "Somehow I missed the point he also made about early learning." She wishes she'd provided more unstructured early learning opportunities for her children. She also took the home-schooling movement's emphasis on phonics to heart and forced her daughter through several phonics programs before they both gave up. "If only I'd realized," she said, "that what my daughter needed was a totally different approach." She finally consulted a reading specialist, but only after she and her daughter were both totally frustrated.

Lack of interaction in discussion and group work with other students

While many critics of home schooling mention lack of social interaction as one of the key disadvantages, this problem can be solved quite easily through a variety of avenues—church, Scouts, park district and community groups, public library activities, and neighborhood playmates. Discussion and group work that takes place in a formal way in the classroom not only helps students learn social skills, but helps them gain a better understanding of the subject matter. Parents can compensate for this disadvantage by becoming learners along with their children. The home-schooling philosophy and curriculum that consists solely of a student working his way through individualized learning packets with little or no discussion and interaction will result in the worst kind of rote learning.

Lack of ready access to special programs (computers, band, chorus, foreign language, athletics) and equipment (science labs, sports facilities)

This is a critical problem, particularly for students in junior high and high school. Serious home schoolers need to be ready to spend money on books, encyclopedias, reference materials, magazines, laboratory equipment, computers, art supplies, and even musical instruments. Many parents budget substantial amounts of money for their program each year since home schoolers need to pay for every outside service their children receive.

Fewer organizational involvement opportunities for parents

One home schooler with whom I spoke, a former public school teacher, spoke somewhat wistfully about missing out on the PTA. "I always thought that someday I would be the PTA president and be a room mother for my kids. I've missed that." She also mentioned feeling left out of the neighborhood camaraderie when parents gather to talk about school and their kids.

Parental stress and burnout

Let's face it. Kids are demanding and sometimes even exasperating. Moms who send their kids off to school have some time to themselves. Kathleen Cruse (mentioned in Chapter Five) home-schooled her four daughters for one year. They were in seventh, fifth, third, and kindergarten. "My kids really loved it, but I burned out. I was with them night and day," she said. Her husband's job took him away from home on many evenings, and she was trying to do everything on her own. Kathleen's experience is duplicated in thousands of homes every year.

A private survey conducted in Washington state found that two-thirds of all home-schooled children had been in that situation for two years or less. A Florida survey found that only 30 percent of the students learning at home had done so during the previous year. Common problems that home-school parents face are lack of success, personality conflicts with children, pressure from friends and family, poor organization, and lack of teaching skills.

What You Need to Know to Be a Successful Home-Schooling Parent

◆

Dr. Harold J. McCurdy of the University of North Carolina studied the childhood lives of twenty historical geniuses in order to discover what they had in common. Three factors emerged: 1) "a high degree of attention focused upon the child by parents and other adults, expressed in intensive educational measures . . . and usually abundant love," 2) "isolation from other children, especially outside the family," and 3) "a rich efflorescence of fantasy, as a reaction to the two preceding conditions."

HAROLD G. MCCURDY, "The Childhood Pattern of Genius" in *Horizon*

If you're well on your way to choosing the home-school option, here are some helpful hints to make your experience a successful one.

Network
Home schoolers seem to have invented networking. There are dozens of groups, newsletters, workshops, and

publishing companies devoted to home schooling. If you are planning to be a successful home schooler, you'll need to get into the network. Talk to people who are presently home-schooling. They are almost universally delighted to talk about what they are doing and share ideas and materials. Also talk with people who have home-schooled and decided it wasn't for them. Try to find parents of older children who can share how their students have succeeded in more advanced schooling or even in life. Hearing success stories like the Colfax's can inspire you to begin and stick with it.

Read

If you're not a voracious reader, then you may have a difficult time home-schooling. There are state laws, newsletters, how-to-do-it books, and curriculum manuals, in addition to dozens of books about spiders, Africa, diamonds, and chemistry that your kids will want to study.

Home schoolers love to write books about their experiences and you'll want to read them all. You will need to be a curious, eager learner, not just to learn yourself, but also to be a good role model for your children. You can't ask them to get excited about home learning if you aren't.

Research

Spend some time looking at different curricula. A curriculum is simply what you want your children to learn. You can use one that someone else has written or even write your own. Once you look at some samples, you'll see that it's not that complicated. Many of the home-schooling resources in the next section contain infor-

mation on where to get copies. Talk to local educators, write
to state departments of education, send for catalogs, and
be creative. That is the reason you're thinking about home
schooling—to do a different and better job than conventional school. Keep a file of clippings and articles about
home schooling. This will be a valuable resource as you
teach. And it will also give you ammunition when the
questions come about why you've chosen this option.

Write
Take pen in hand and set forth what you believe about
education. Make yourself verbalize exactly why you want
to home-school. Examine your motives and write them
down. If it's been awhile, you need to know what it feels
like to write. You will be asking your children to write for
you every day. You need to begin to model writing as well
as reading. Keep a daily journal where you record your
thoughts, ideas, and frustrations about home schooling.
Who knows? You may have the beginnings of a book.

Believe
If you're going to be a successful home schooler you have
to believe in your own ability to teach your children. You
also have to believe strongly that you have made the
right choice. That is why researching and reading *before*
you make the choice is so important. There will be many
who will try to change your mind. You need to be convinced of the "rightness" of your decision.

Plan
If you don't write it down, you probably won't accomplish it. One home schooler put it this way: "Make

a list. Don't dream." Setting both short- and long-term goals is very important. The first year your goal will be just "getting started." But as you and your "school" mature, begin to think in terms of setting goals in each of the developmental areas: spiritual, social, emotional, physical, psychological, and intellectual. Think globally about your goals. Don't be tied down merely to the specific curricular expectations.

Get ready for the real world

Experienced home schoolers with whom I spoke emphasized the importance of preparing your child to face a conventional schooling experience. If you know that at some point along the way your child will transfer, plan early. Most home schoolers choose to make this transition near the junior-high or high-school age because of the challenge of teaching more complex subject matter. Helping your child develop skills he or she will need to succeed in the formal setting can help make the transition a smooth one.

Relax

Some home schoolers are very intense. They pack so much into every day that it's no wonder they burn out and take their children with them. To a mother who asked about how to prevent burnout, Micki Colfax answered: "You've probably been taking yourself too seriously. Back off and give yourself and the children some space—physical, emotional, and intellectual."[4]

Enjoy

Any time you spend with your children is precious. I am envious of the home schoolers I have talked with. The close and special relationships they share with their children are notable. If you choose to home-school your child, make this part of your motto: *Enjoy every minute.*

---◆---

In the last two decades, Christian home-schooling has made important strides. Unlike the Christian schools, home-schooling has broken away from the public school's inefficient structure and developed an approach to education that honors the biblical principles of education.
GREGG HARRIS in *Schooling Choices: An Examination of Private, Public, & Home Education*

Resources to Help You Be a More Informed Home-School Parent

The following books, organizations, and free and inexpensive materials will help you become a more knowledgeable and effective home-school parent.

Books

The following list is by no means a complete one. These resources will lead you to others. Home-schooling advocates write wonderful books. For some reason they are much more exciting than public and Christian school books. Perhaps that is because the truly committed home-schooler is experiencing firsthand the joys of teaching and wants everyone else to do the same.

☐ Colfax, David and Micki
Homeschooling for Excellence
Mountain House Press, 1987
The story of the Colfax family's home-schooling experience. As noted earlier, their sons have all attended Harvard University and were home-schooled on the Colfax goat ranch in California.

☐ Gorder, Cheryl
Home Schools: An Alternative
Blue Bird Publishing, 1990
The third edition of this helpful volume contains a little bit of everything—resources, rational, and reading lists. Add it to your library of home-schooling books.

☐ Harris, Gregg
The Christian Home-School
Wolgemuth & Hyatt, 1987
A thoughtful and practical book by the founder and director of Christian Life Workshops. Contains a sound philosophy of home schooling as well as helps for those wanting to get started.

☐ Hendrickson, Borg
Home-School: Taking the First Step
Mountain Meadow Press, 1989
If I were starting a home school, this book would be

my bible. Contains everything you need to know written in a clear and understandable fashion. The resource sections (Regulations and Procedures, Support Groups, Readings for Parents, Home-School Curriculum Suppliers, and Teaching Materials) are the best I've seen.

Another helpful book by Hendrickson is *How to Write a Low Cost/No Cost Curriculum For Your Home-School Child* (Mountain Meadow Press, 1990).

☐ Holt, John
How Children Fail
Delacorte Press, 1982
The late John Holt is one of the founding gurus of the secular home-schooling movement. Holt's approach to home schooling offers a "real" alternative to structured schools. Other books by Holt include *Instead of Education: Ways to Help People Do Things Better* (E.P. Dutton & Co., Inc., 1976), and *How Children Learn* (Delacorte, 1982).

☐ Lopez, Diane
Teaching Children
Crossway Books, 1988
This is the third book in a series designed to bring the educational philosophies of Charlotte Mason, an English educator whose books have for many years been out of print, to the contemporary home schooler. Susan Schaeffer Macaulay's *For the Children's Sake* (Crossway Books, 1984) and *Books Children Love* by Elizabeth Wilson (Crossway Books, 1987) were the

first two. Read the books as a set for maximum effectiveness.

❏ Moore, Raymond and Dorothy
Home-Grown Kids: A Practical Handbook for Teaching Your Child at Home
Word Books, 1981
The Moores have authored numerous books (*Home-Spun Schools*, Word, 1982 and *Home-Style Teaching: A Handbook for Parents and Teachers,* Word, 1984) and have been the front-runners in Christian home-schooling for years. Their successful experience with their grown children and their educational credentials make what they have to say worth listening to. Their most recent book is *Home-School Burnout: What It Is. What Causes It. And How to Cure It.* (Wolgemuth and Hyatt, 1988).

❏ Pride, Mary
The Big Book of Home Learning
Crossway Books, 1986
Before you know it, you'll have spent an hour or two with this wonderful resource book containing materials and ideas for home schoolers. Mary Pride's witty reviews and honest appraisals are fun reading even if you don't intend to buy anything. *The Next Big Book of Home Learning* (1987) contains sources on a variety of additional subject matter areas like mythology and logic. A second edition, *The New Big Book of Home Learning* (1988), contains additional resources and up-dated price lists.

◻ Shackelford, Luanne and Susan White
A Survivor's Guide to Home Schooling
Crossway Books, 1988
Two experienced home-schooling moms share their humorous, but helpful hints for making your home school a success.

◻ Wade, Theodore E.
The Home-School Manual
Gazelle Publications, 1984
Contains a great deal of helpful information about beginning your own home school.

◻ Wallace, Nancy
Better Than School
Larson Publications, 1983
A firsthand story of one family's home-schooling experiences.

Organizations

The following organizations/publishers provide information about establishing home schools as well as support for parents currently engaged in home schooling. Write to them for further information. Where indicated, newsletters and brochures are available.

◻ The Chalkboard
Box 1043
Vashon Island, WA 98070
This is a publication of the home-taught kids special interest group of American Mensa, Ltd.

❏ Christian Home Schools
  8731 N.E. Everett St.,
  Portland, OR 97220
  They publish a resource guide by Sue Welch.

❏ Christian Life Workshops
  Gregg Harris & Family
  182 S.E. Kane Rd.
  Gresham, OR 97080
  Christian Life Workshops is the household ministry
  of the author. He conducts The Home Schooling
  Workshop nationally, in both live and video-taped
  versions. He also publishes *Family Restoration
  Quarterly* for alumni and friends. Many materials are
  available by mail order. To receive a catalog and
  sample of the *Quarterly,* enclose one dollar for postage
  and handling.

❏ Holt Associates
  2269 Massachusetts Avenue
  Cambridge, MA 02140
  617-864-3100
  The magazine "Growing without Schooling" is published by Holt Associates, Inc., a clearinghouse of
  information about children and home schooling. Sub-
  scriptions are available by writing to the above address. A home-schooling resource list is available for
  $1.00 and a SASE.

❏ Home-School Coalition
  P.O. Box 835105
  Richardson, TX 75083

"Home Education: Is It Working?" a booklet citing positive home-school research is available by writing.

❒ The Home School Legal Defense Association
P.O. Box 159
Highway 9 at Route 781
Paeonian Springs, VA 22129
703-882-3838
Fax 703-882-3628
This organization, headed by Michael Farris, provides legal assistance for home-schooling parents for an annual fee of $100. An application and sample newsletter will be mailed upon request. If you can do so, please include one dollar for postage and handling. Available publications include Home Schooling and the Law by Michael P. Farris.

❒ The Moore Foundation
Box 1
Camas, WA 98607
206-835-2736
Raymond and Dorothy Moore, founding father and mother of the home-schooling movement, publish a bi-monthly newsletter and offer dozens of helpful books and pamphlets. The Moore Formula for Home Schooling is the best place to begin if you decide to home-school.

❒ National Home-School Association
P.O. Box 58746
Seattle, WA 98138-1746
206-432-1544

The National Home-School Association was founded in 1988. Its primary aims are to promote individual freedom and choice in education, to serve families who choose to home-school, and to inform the general public about home education. Membership in NHA is open to everyone and includes the quarterly newsletter, voting privileges for all elections, and access to service programs. A special packet is offered for new home schoolers.

❐ National Home Research Education Institute
25 W Cremona Street
Seattle, WA 98119
206-283-3650
The president of National Home Research Education Institute is Dr. Brian Ray, an education professor at Seattle-Pacific University and editor of *Home-school Researcher,* a quarterly journal. Dr. Ray also publishes the "Home-Centered Learning Annotated Bibliography."

❐ The Teaching Home
P.O. Box 20219
Portland, OR 97220-0219
503-253-9633
A bimonthly magazine that provides information and support to Christian home-schooling families and organizations. Excellent, well-written articles and resources for all educators.

8

Evaluating
Your Options

*The direction in which education starts
a man will determine
his future life.*
PLATO

*U*nless you're the kind of person who reads a book in reverse, then you've already completed Steps One through Four. For many of you, the hardest part of the job may already be completed. However, if you love to gather facts and information, but have a difficult time making final decisions, then the hardest part of the task is still ahead. Step Five consists of looking at the specific options open to you and then making the final decision. If your child is still a preschooler, you may have several years to cogitate. But if you need to make a decision before September, then you still have several important things to do.

Now that you understand the strengths and weaknesses of each of the three school options, you're ready to do an in-depth evaluation of the specific options open to you. What does your neighborhood public school look like? How does the Christian school measure up? What would your home school look like if you set it up tomorrow? Remember the warning I gave you in Chapter One. You won't find perfection anywhere. You'll have to make some compromises whatever you choose. The kindergarten teacher at the Christian school is absolutely marvelous, but there is no art or music program. You're all set to home-school, but suddenly remember that you'll have to teach math and science. The public school principal is an absolute dynamo, but your child's teacher for next year looks like she retired in 1957. The following sections will help you evaluate each of the options to determine which one is right for you.

How to Evaluate Your Public School

> Every education teaches a philosophy; if not by design then by suggestion, by implication, by atmosphere. Every part of that education has a connection with every other part. If it does not all combine to convey some general view of life, it is not an education at all.
> G.K. CHESTERTON

The evaluation of your local public school is complicated by the fact that you are also evaluating a school district. Even if a district enjoys an overall excellent reputation, individual schools within the district can vary considerably. The building principal, individual teachers, and parental involvement are all factors that can "make or break" a school.

Some families who are committed to the public schools as an educational choice buy a home solely because of its location in a specific school district or within a certain local attendance boundary. Sometimes they want their children to play for a winning football coach or be a part of a state championship speech team. Others believe that their children's chances of getting into the "best" college will increase when they attend a selected school. But even when a district or school has a good reputation, it pays to evaluate carefully.

Checklist for evaluating a public school district

- **Expenditures.** Find out how much is being spent on the average per child. This figure, called the *per pupil expenditure,* can tell you many things about a school district. Just because a district has the highest *per pupil expenditure* in a general geographic area doesn't necessarily mean it offers the best education, but an expenditure level that is significantly lower than neighboring districts needs investigation. It may be that the district is fiscally well managed, or it could be that the district either doesn't believe in spending any money beyond the basic program or doesn't have the money to spend.

- **Taxes.** You will want to know the amount of the assessed valuation per child. This figure is determined by adding up the value of all of the property within the school district and dividing it by the number of students who attend school there. The higher the number the better, but you'll need to compare it with others in your state to make a meaningful judgment. A high *per pupil assessed valuation* means that local home owners can pay lower tax rates and generate the same number of dollars as their neighbors with a lower assessed valuation. But the important question really is, how much is your annual property tax bill?

- **Test scores and other data.** Many states require school districts to report their annual test scores, student dropout rate, and other important demographic data to the public each year. Other measures that will tell you how well the schools are doing include the number of National Merit Semifinalists, the percentage of students who go on to college, and work placement of graduates.

- **Facilities.** How do the buildings in the school district look? Are they attractive, safe, and well maintained? Do they enhance the neighborhoods in which they are located?

- **Publicity.** Read the local newspapers and find out what kinds of articles are featured about the public schools. Is there positive news about good things that are happening in the schools? Are there stories about students who have won awards and received recognition? Or, is the news about strikes, school closings, and declining test scores?

- **Administration.** Make an appointment to talk with a central office administrator. Perhaps the superintendent won't be available, but talk with an assistant superintendent or curriculum director. Business managers can give you another perspective on how the district is run. If you can't find someone who is willing to talk with you about the school district, you'd better eliminate this district from your list.

- **School board members.** Call up a local newspaper or the library to find out who the local school board members are. Interview one or two of them to find out what they believe about education and why they think the school district is a good one. If a school board member doesn't have ten reasons why you should attend the local schools, put up a "for sale" sign.

- **Reputation.** Talk with local community college and/or university education professors. They will often give you an unbiased viewpoint based on experiences their student teachers have had in the schools. Real-estate agents who serve a variety of communities can also give comparative information. If the office serves a single community, however, you will more likely receive a biased opinion.

Checklist for evaluating your local public school
While the reputation of an entire district is certainly an important factor in whether or not you choose to send your child to the public school, that information alone is not enough. You must do an in-depth evaluation of the local school.

- **Administrative leadership.** Talking with the building principal is the first step in your school evaluation. Research is very clear on the importance of instructional leadership by the principal. If he or she doesn't have answers to your questions, is unwilling to introduce you to teachers, and can't make arrangements for you to take a school tour or visit a classroom, keep looking.

- **Classroom teachers.** Ask to visit a classroom or two at your child's grade level. A quick look in the room can tell you a great deal. Does this look like the kind of place your child would want to spend nine months? Even more revealing than an actual classroom visit, however, is information from parents whose children have spent a year in that classroom. The reputations of classroom teachers spread quickly through the neighborhood. Do you hear more horror stories than successes? Neighborhood gossip is not always the best source of objective information about the schools, but hearing the same "horror" story from several different individuals should raise a red flag of warning.

- **School goals and mission.** Ask to see a written copy of the school goals or mission. This statement will give you a good idea as to the focus and philosophy of the school staff. Do they believe that all students can learn? Do they have a set of outcomes that all students are expected to master?

Education has for its object the formation of character.
HERBERT SPENCER

- **Building climate.** Many people think of the temperature and weather conditions when they read the word "climate." But in educational jargon, this word means how things look and feel when you walk through a school building. Do children and adults look involved and engaged in teaching and learning? Are people friendly and open? Do you see student work displayed in the halls? Does the secretary growl at you when you interrupt her typing, or do you feel welcome and at home even though you've only been there for a few minutes?

- **Parental involvement.** Find out if parents are welcome in the school. Do they volunteer in classrooms and the library? Do they tutor students who need extra help? What kind of parent organization exists, and what projects have they undertaken to improve the school? Is there a committee of parents that meets regularly with the principal to give him or her feedback and suggestions about the school?

- **Building appearance.** Whether a building is old or new doesn't matter. But how it is cared for is *definitely* important. The pride a staff takes in the physical appearance of their building often reflects a deeper, more important commitment to education and children.

- **Curriculum.** What will your child learn? What kinds of textbooks will be used? Is there a statement of outcomes that is specific to that school building? Besides the "basics," what other subjects are taught? What subjects are mandated by the state? What kinds of programs are used for sex and drug education? How much time is spent on each of the subjects during a typical week?

- **Instructional methodologies.** Is this a traditional school where all of the desks are in rows? Do teachers use cooperative groups and less structured teaching methods? Are all the classrooms the same, or is there an opportunity for teachers to be creative and "do their own thing"?

- **Electives and extracurricular activities.** Once the dismissal bell rings, are there other opportunities for students to be involved? Student Council? Sports? Music lessons? Are these activities free?

- **Library media center.** Ask to visit the media center and find out how often your child will be able to use it. Find out if students can use video equipment or check out magazines.

- **Computer lab.** Computers are the new technology in schools, and computers are essential tools for academic success. What opportunities exist for your child to become computer literate?

- **Class size.** While the research on class size does not always agree on the exact optimum number, most educators agree that teachers can give more individual attention when class size is smaller. This is particularly important in the early elementary grades. Find out what the average district class size is and what the district generally does if a large number of new students enroll in a class or school.

- **Tracking and grouping.** A school's philosophy on tracking students (putting them in a group based on their ability and then designing their educational program for K-12 based on that group) can often determine what educational opportunities your child will have. If your child is in the "top group," he'll probably receive plenty of enrichment and special attention, but putting a child in the lowest reading group in first grade may lower his self-esteem and make it difficult for him to be a successful student. Many schools (even junior high and high schools) are recognizing the benefits of large group instruction and are doing much less grouping and tracking.

Education is the best provision for old age.
ARISTOTLE

- **Homework.** What is the school's policy with regard to homework? How much homework per night can parents expect at the different grade levels? Is homework just busywork?

- **Textbooks.** Is there a basic reading series or can teachers select novels and other materials? (This practice may make it difficult for parents to monitor what is being used in the classroom.) What is the textbook selection process and how can the parent view textbooks for different courses and grade levels?

- **Guidance and support services.** What happens if your child has a problem in school? What kinds of support services are available to help him?

- **Communication.** How can you find out what is happening at school? Is there a monthly newsletter? Do teachers send home weekly notes? Can you drop in whenever you want to ask questions and talk? When do teachers hold conferences with parents?

- **Safety.** Will you need to worry about your child when he or she is walking to and from school or playing on the playground? What kinds of supervision (playground, crossing guards) are available and when?

- **Discipline.** What are the behavioral expectations of the school? What are the rules? What will happen to your child if he breaks the rules or gets in trouble? What is the principal's philosophy of discipline?

- **Transportation.** How will your child get to school? Will he have a long bus ride? Will there be safety patrols to help him cross at busy streets?

- **Unique features.** In my experience, every school has something special about it that defines the school as unique—programs, people, events, history. Find out what is special about the school you are investigating. If no one can tell you what is special, keep looking for another school.

Maybe you won't have time to find out the answers to all of these questions. And maybe even discovering a problem or two isn't going to make a big difference in your decision. After all, we did say that nothing was perfect. But being forewarned about a potential problem can often make the difference between a spectacular school year and a mediocre one for your child.

Here's an example. Perhaps you've been impressed by the school principal and the building. There is a warm and friendly climate and the academic goals seem just right for your child. You've just about decided that this is the school. But you've heard there is a big difference between the two third-grade teachers. One is highly structured and organized. Her class is run like a finely tuned machine. Discipline is firm but fair and there is no nonsense. The basics are emphasized. In the classroom across the hall, the other teacher is more individualistic. His sense of humor is somewhat offbeat and he uses more creative teaching methods. The class may not always be quiet or on the same textbook page.

After reading Chapter Three, you have a pretty good idea of which teacher will best meet the needs of your child. Why keep that vital information a secret? Why not make a suggestion to the principal? Of course you won't demand or insist. But a subtle hint can't hurt and can often "assist" the administrator in placing your child. "My Johnny learns best in a highly structured environment." Or, "My Sarah is quite an individual. Sometimes her sense of humor is a little off the wall."

How to Evaluate Your Christian School

Train a child in the way he should go, and when he is old he will not turn from it.

Proverbs 22:6

Evaluating the Christian school option is even more complicated than evaluating the public school. In addition to *all* of the above questions, there's a whole new set of questions specifically for the Christian school.

Checklist for evaluating a Christian school

- **Location.** Many parents send their children to Christian schools that are located in other communities. Does the location of the school make a difference in your decision? How will your child get to school if your car breaks down or you get ill?

- **Administrator.** The Christian school principal can assume an even more important role than his public school counterpart. He or she usually has more autonomy in how the building is run than the public school principal. This individual's faith, philosophy of discipline and education, and problem-solving skills are critical for the success of the school. Getting off to a good start with the principal is always important, but doubly so in the Christian school.

- **Teachers.** Unless the school is large, there may be only one teacher per grade level in the elementary school. Try to visit in this teacher's classroom and talk with him or her. At the very least do a little research by talking to other parents. Some parents would never think of questioning the wisdom, judgment, and teaching credentials of the Christian school teacher, or any teacher for that matter. Their philosophy is that "my child has been placed in this room for a reason and he's going to make it no matter what." Parents on the other end of the continuum are constantly measuring, judging, and examining their child's teacher. They are ready to ask for a transfer at a moment's notice. A position somewhere in the middle is probably the best. All teachers have their idiosyncracies. What drives you crazy may be exactly what your child loves. I thought my son's third grade teacher was a touch "spacy." He said she loved boys and did wonderful science experiments. If you're evaluating high school teachers, ask about their levels of experience. While new, young teachers bring an enthusiasm and excitement to teaching, constant turnover and a steady diet of brand-new teachers could spell academic trouble for your child.

- **Association membership.** What affiliations does the school have with outside organizations that provide support, structure, information, and teacher training? What Christian school association do they belong to?

- **Class size.** What is the average class size? What is the size of the class your child will be in? Sometimes Christian schools have wonderfully small class sizes. In some cases they are impossibly high. This is an important question to ask, particularly if your child is gifted or needs special help. For that matter, most kids don't thrive well in large classes. No amount of Christian education can compensate for spending first grade with over twenty-five students in the class.

- **Integrated faith and learning.** How do the faculty members integrate faith and learning? If you are choosing the Christian school especially for its religious emphasis, then this is a critical question. Is the integration simply prayer before class begins and an occasional Bible class, or have teachers and administrators truly developed an integrated curriculum? Press both the administrator and teachers for specific examples of how this takes place at various grade levels and in various subjects.

> The very spring and root of honesty and virtue lies in good education.
> PLUTARCH

- **Curriculum/textbooks.** Do teachers make up their own? Is there a denominational curriculum that is followed? What are students expected to learn and what kinds of academic standards are upheld?

- **Denomination.** Is the school associated with a specific denomination or set of religious beliefs? Are these compatible with your own?

- **Philosophy/beliefs.** Truly distinctive Christian schools are hard to find. A statement of philosophy should be comprehensive and thoroughly developed. Some schools have borrowed a secular statement and tried to modify it or "Christianize" it. Others don't have any philosophy at all. Beware of such a school. They probably haven't really decided what they are trying to do. Their philosophy should include the school's beliefs about children and learning. Do they believe that all kids can learn? Or, will they cut you loose and cast you adrift if your child doesn't measure up to their standards?

- **Funding/tuition.** Where does the school get its money? Of course you'll be paying tuition, but that won't cover all of the operating expenses. Do they have wealthy benefactors? Are there endowment funds? Or, do they live from hand to mouth, with parents wondering from year to year if school will open in September? What will you be expected to pay and how can you pay it? Are there financial-aid packages? Are students expected to work if they receive aid? Where and when do they work? Are parents expected to fund-raise and make other contributions?

- **History.** How long has the school been in existence? What is the track record of their graduates as they go on to either high school or higher education? Do these results mesh with the expectations you have for your child?

- **Expectations for parents.** What does the school expect from you with regard to time and money? Find out up front so that there are no surprises later on. Will you need to serve on committees, assist teachers on projects, or work on fund-raising drives?

- **Makeup of student body.** What does the student body look like? If the school is associated with a church, what percentage of the families are church members? Are there any minorities? How many students receive financial aid?

- **Testing and evaluation.** How will you know that your child is learning? Is there a program of annual standardized testing? Which tests are given and how are they reported? How do the scores measure up to the best public schools in the area?

- **Visitation rights.** Can you visit classrooms by appointment? Parents can visit public school classrooms by appointment at any time. This practice is important in all schools.

- **Special programs for gifted, learning disabled.** What if your child has a problem? What services can the school provide?

- **School rules/dress code/pledge.** What are the expectations with regard to what your child can wear to school? Is there a specific set of behavioral standards that a student must follow (smoking, drinking, movies, dancing)?

- **Unique features.** Find out what is distinctive about the school. It may be its long list of notable Christian graduates. Or perhaps it has an unusual ministry in the community. Maybe it helps kids succeed who have had problems learning anywhere else. Find out what is special about the school. If there is nothing notable, choose another.

How to Evaluate Your Home School

> The object of education is to prepare the young to
> educate themselves throughout their lives.
> ROBERT MAYNARD HUTCHINS

Evaluating the home-school option will be somewhat different than evaluating conventional school settings. By their nature, home schools are unique, each one as individual as the parent who runs it. If you're close to choosing the home-schooling option, begin to think about what your specific school will look like. Will it be different and better than either the public school or the Christian school? What will you offer your child that he or she can't get anywhere else? What will make it distinctive from the Johnsons' Home School across the street?

Let me give an example. In my interviews with a variety of home schoolers, each one has shown or told me the special things that make me want to send my child to their "school."

The Wienekes' learning process is seldom confined to textbooks and manuals. They hatch chickens, sew clothing, play "store," and plan family meals. Their "school room" is filled with interesting "stuff." At the Armstrongs, there is a strong academic approach. The teacher wants to make sure she prepares her student for a competitive high school experience. Across town at the Lanes', character building is an important emphasis of each day. They are also learning how to do "chores." Each of these home-schools has a slightly different educational philosophy. You will need to have your philosophy clearly in mind if you want to be a successful home schooler.

Checklist for Evaluating Your Home School

- **Curriculum.** Your curriculum is what you will be teaching. In conventional school settings we have three kinds of curriculum: *the explicit, the implicit, and the null.* The *explicit* curriculum is what we say we teach—our guides and textbooks. The *implicit* curriculum is the hidden curriculum. That's the one that worries people about the public schools—the values and ideas that somehow slip in unnoticed until it's too late. The *null* curriculum is all the stuff we don't teach, and in the public schools we don't teach a lot that people think we should. So as you think about choosing your curriculum, remember those three categories.

- **Philosophy.** What do you believe about what kids should learn and how they should learn it? Should they have any say in the matter? What part does discipline play in learning? How should faith and learning be integrated? What is the role of education? Is schooling the same as education? What subjects are the most important? When should a child learn to read? These and dozens of other questions need to be answered before one can do a good job of evaluating the home-schooling option.

- **Teaching methodology.** Most beginning teachers teach the way they were taught. It's comfortable and secure. And they know it works, because they turned out all right. Didn't they? But there are dozens of teaching approaches that can bring variety and interest to the home school.

The most common approach is the traditional one where teachers teach out of a manual of some sort, students and teachers discuss and interact, and students complete assignments to demonstrate what they have learned. A second curricular approach is independent and self-directed. It is often called programmed learning. Students read through materials, fill out workbooks and then move on to the next lesson. The third approach is what I like to call "discovery" learning. All of the subjects can be taught while studying a specific topic like Indians or insects. Instead of having separate lessons in reading, math, and writing, there are many hands-on activities all centered around the subject, and students take a much greater responsibility for determining what they will learn. The best conventional classrooms combine all three approaches, finding that always doing things the same way can get boring and dull. Home schoolers find this to be true also. But you will need to decide what your major emphasis will be in order to purchase materials.

Finding out about the various teaching approaches and trying out one or two can help you decide whether home schooling is for you. After all, if you're going to do this, you want to be the best teacher you can be. Borg Hendrickson offers one of the best lists I've seen of alternate teaching methods.[1] Manipulative learning, thematic lessons, competency-based, diagnostic-prescriptive, and child-directed are just a few.

I am not willing that this discussion should close without mention of the value of a true teacher. Give me a log hut, with only a simple bench, Mark Hopkins on one end and I on the other, and you may have all the building, apparatus and libraries without him.
JAMES ABRAM GARFIELD

- **Lesson plans, scheduling, and calendars.** The key to successful home schooling is to know where you want to go. If you're not the kind of person who thrives on organization and structure, you can compensate. But most of the experts agree that you need to have a plan and that you need to follow it.

- **Materials.** Developing and selling materials for home schoolers is a burgeoning industry. Mary Pride's catalogs are a wonderful example of that. You could spend thousands of dollars on materials if you had an unlimited budget. How will you decide what to buy? Where will you buy it?

- **Evaluation.** A critical component of a successful home school is an evaluation program of some sort. Standardized tests aren't the sole criterion for how well your child is learning, but they offer some comparison of how your child measures up to his age-mates across the country. Just as important as the standardized tests, however, are the mini-evaluations that you build in along the way. If one of your curricular goals is to teach values to your children, then figure out a way to measure how successful you have been. Are your children kind to their siblings? To the neighborhood children? To their pets? If your curricular goal is to teach letter writing, then your evaluation will be the ability of your child to write a letter to Grandma without any help from Mom.

- **Affiliation/support groups/correspondence courses.** Home schoolers need support from one another. Investigate and determine where you're going to find that support. Will you join a group? Will you subscribe to a newsletter? Will you become part of a correspondence school?

- **Social opportunities.** Your child will need social opportunities and so will you. Keep looking until you find a friend for your child. You can't be all things to your child and he/she will need age-mates to talk with on the phone or play with in the park. As an only child until the age of four, I grew up in the country. I was a social child and could hardly wait to take the bus to school where I could meet some other children. I had only read about other children in books and dearly wanted to play the games and have the fun that groups of kids seemed to have. I was not disappointed and shudder to think how miserable I would have made my poor mother had I not been able to get out of the house.

Determine how you will build social opportunities into your home-school schedule. Will it be park district, library, church, 4-H? What organizations and programs can meet that need?

- **Individual profile.** Do a good job of self-examination and determine what, if anything, might hold you back from being an effective home schooler. Is it your lack of organization? The fact that you don't really read or write that much? Perhaps you are a procrastinator? Maybe your spiritual life won't stand up to the scrutiny of daily living with your child?

At this point, you should be ready to make your choice. It's not as scary as it might seem. Just remember—into the life of every child and parent a little rain will fall. Whether or not you re-evaluate your decision and choose to change is the topic for discussion in Chapter Nine.

Let early education be a sort of amusement; you will then be better able to find out the natural bent.
PLATO

9

Choosing to Change

Two years ago, when we realized that Becky's progress had come to a complete stop, we made a terribly difficult decision. Now it's clear to us that changing her mode of schooling was a wise choice. Becky—and the rest of the family—feel and function much better now.

ANONYMOUS

*H*ow do you know if your child needs a change? How can you tell whether the problem is one your child will have in any school setting, or is specific to his present classroom or school? Step Six in the process of choosing the right schooling option for your child is to *monitor and evaluate.* Many parents have the philosophy that adversity builds character and that no matter how bad the teacher or the school is, their children will learn to live with it. That's what I call "the teacher is always right" syndrome. Other parents react to every whim of their offspring and are subject to their children's clever manipulation. That's "the child is always right" syndrome. In many cases, there's a little bit of both in every problem, but, in some cases, a genuine problem exists and must be solved for a child to learn and grow.

Our dinner conversations were no longer happy and lighthearted. In the past I would talk about the funny things that had happened during my day as an elementary school principal—the student who brought a dead frog in a bottle to class or the deer that wandered onto our playground from a nearby forest preserve. My daughter would talk about letters she'd received from one of her dozens of pen pals. My husband would talk about the rise and fall of the Dow-Jones. And Patrick, our sixth grader, would talk about everything under the sun. But lately his conversations had focused on only one topic, his teacher. He told horror stories of her gloomy moods and bad tempers. He recounted the number of students reduced to tears by her vicious attacks. He personally never seemed to be the object of Mrs. McCray's* vitriolic tongue; he merely observed her with fear and trembling, wondering when she would turn on him. We tried the approach that most parents take when confronted by a school problem: we told him to ignore it, and it would go away.

But every night at dinner and bedtime, the worries and complaints would pour forth. After several weeks, I decided to check out his story with a number of parents I knew whose students were in the class. Perhaps Patrick had an overactive imagination and things were not really as bad as he described them. But my research revealed that he was accurate. Sharon's mother said that Mrs. McCray had reduced her daughter to tears over a

*Not her real name

lost homework assignment. When I called Matt's mom, she quizzed him while I was still on the line. "Yes," she reported, "Matt says the same thing. Mrs. McCray even whacked someone over the head with a rolled-up newspaper today." I was beginning to discover that the situation was even worse than Patrick had described it.

The next morning, I called the school principal and told him how unhappy we all were. I asked him what could be done. Fortunately he was a reasonable person. He didn't argue and tell me I didn't know what I was talking about. The principal didn't defend the teacher and her actions; he simply asked me what I would like to see happen in this situation. So Patrick and I talked it over. He thought he'd like to transfer out of the class. It meant leaving some of his best friends, but even friends couldn't compensate for seven more months of Mrs. McCray. We made such a move and finished the year without incident.

Not every administrator is willing to make changes. And not every problem can be solved so easily. There are times when a more radical change is needed, a totally different schooling choice.

But before you think about choosing to change, let's look at some reasons for staying right where you are.

When You Should Make the Decision to Stay

Stay where you are when everyone agrees on the problem and is willing to work on a solution
As wise as we often think we are, we sometimes don't know a good thing when we see it. Before you rush off into some unknown situation, give all the players a

chance to work on a solution to the problem. If you're having a problem with a teacher and she agrees to make some changes, give her a chance. If the administrator or school board is responsive, be gracious and admit that you were premature in your judgments.

Stay where you are when you think the problem is your child's and he has the ability to do something about it where he is

If the problem is your child's problem and *only* his problem, then moving to a new setting will not solve the problem. Moving will confirm for your child that if he doesn't want to "shape up" or conform, he just has to complain and Super Mom or Super Dad will come to the rescue. Figure out if your child is the one who needs to change rather than everyone else. Sometimes children need a fresh start, but give them every opportunity to solve the problem where it started. They will feel better about themselves if they can.

Stay where you are if it's close to the end of the school year

Don't make a change near the end of a school year. Everyone tends to get tired and discouraged after nearly nine months of hard work. Talk about the decision over the summer when life is less pressured. Everything may not look so bleak when the weather is warmer.

Stay where you are until you've had a chance to sleep on it for a week or two, pray about it, and talk it over with several people whose judgment you trust

Only if your child's life is in danger does the decision to change a school need to be made overnight. Give yourself

158

the benefit of prayer, thought, and discussion before you make a decision to move.

Stay where you are if it appears that your child is manipulating the situation to get what he wants without a sincere desire to change
Some children are masters of manipulation. They know that if they can convince their parents that the problem belongs to someone else, they won't have to "face the music."

Stay where you are when you're in the middle of a family crisis
Making a decision about schooling for your child while you're in the middle of a family crisis is a big mistake. There might not even be a schooling crisis once the family problem is resolved. Be careful to determine if schooling is really the problem or if some other problem is masquerading as a schooling problem. Often a pastor or family counselor can help you see the situation more clearly.

When Should You Leave the Public School?

◆

It is critical . . . that we distinguish between creative conflict and negative dissonance between family and school. The former is inevitable in changing society and adaptive to the development and socialization of children. The latter is dysfunctional to child growth and acculteration and degrading to families, communities and cultures . . . Conflict is potentially constructive as a way of clarifying and resolving differences in culture and ideology between families and schools.

SARA LAWRENCE LIGHTFOOT, *Worlds Apart: Relationships Between Families and Schools*

Kathy and Lyle Morrow believe in the public schools. They both have dedicated their lives to teaching there. Their son attended the public schools until he was in sixth grade. But they wish they had transferred him to a Christian school far sooner. They spent too much time thinking that everything would work out all right. What they didn't count on was the power of a group of kids to take over the class and the school and to terrorize everyone, including the teacher and the principal. Their son lost time both emotionally and academically because of his experience.

Susan R.'s mother also has a sad story to tell. Her freshman daughter got mixed up with the wrong crowd and turned to drugs. The mother made the decision to get her daughter out of the environment immediately.

There are eight reasons to transfer from the public school.

Transfer when your child is constantly harassed, bullied, or is in danger

The problem of playground bullies exists everywhere, but if teachers and administrators will not face up to the problem and deal with it, you as a parent are powerless to change things. You can teach your child strategies for dealing with bullies, but without effective adult support, his life will be miserable if he has become a victim. Children who have different values or are sensitive or gifted can often be singled out for verbal, if not physical, abuse.

Transfer when your child has become involved with the wrong peer group

Your child's friends will become more important to him with each passing year of school. If your child has friends that you feel are influencing him to act in unacceptable ways, then do everything in your power to get your child away from these friends. Be reasonable in your judgments, however. My children have many friends with strange clothing, weird hairdos, unusual lifestyles, and bizarre tastes in music and reading, but that doesn't necessarily make them a bad influence on my children. But if you can document a decline in your child's motivation, attitudes, respect for family rules, and moral standards, that is genuine cause for alarm.

Transfer when your child is regularly being exposed to drugs, sex, and violence

If your children have to worry about drugs, sex, and violence as part of their daily environment, they will have little time to concentrate on learning. And neither will anyone else.

Transfer when your child is failing with no hope of rescue

No child should fail in school. There's no reason for it. Find a place where he or she can get the kind of help and

attention that is needed. Tackle problems like this very
early. High-school failure, unless it is sudden (or isolated
to a class or two), did not begin in high school. It probably
began in first grade. Pay attention when your child gets
failing grades. Something serious is wrong—either with
him, with his teacher, with his parents, or with his
school. Find out what the problem is and *get help*.

Transfer when you object to everything that is done
There are some Christians who have their children in
the public schools and spend all of their time criticizing
everything that happens. They are just lying in wait,
ready to find a library book with a swearword, a course
that might introduce their child to some humanistic
value, or a teacher with an alternate lifestyle. Your
children will be much happier if they don't constantly
have to worry about every little thing that happens in
school. Parents of public school students need to trust
the judgment of their children. If you can't do that, you're
better off in another setting.

***Transfer when you have an unresolved conflict
with the school administrator and teachers***
If you're at war with your child's teacher or the school
principal, try to find a way to resolve that conflict. If it
can't be resolved, then transfer. Children know when the
people who are important in their lives aren't getting
along. They suffer when their parents disagree over
things and they also suffer when their parents and
teachers don't agree. Children are masters at using these

differences to do exactly what they want. So if there's a problem, do something about it. You must be able to wholeheartedly support your schools.

There are some exceptions to this rule, however. At the high-school level my children have had teachers whose methods I might have questioned or whose characters I might have criticized. My children and I discussed those issues together, and at that point in their lives, they were able to deal with the situations as adults. I still let my children know that disagreeing with a teacher's methods or his lifestyle didn't give them an excuse to do poorly in the class. I expected that they would do their best.

Transfer when the teachers are poor and no one will do anything about it
There are poor teachers everywhere. Some of them are very nice people. They just can't teach. If your child gets one of those people and there's nothing you can do to get your child into another classroom, look for another school. Nothing should stand in the way of your child learning. That is why he is in school. There's too much to accomplish to waste a year in an unproductive situation.

Transfer when your child is not achieving to his potential because of a lack of programs and services
If your child has a special need and no one will address that need, then find another school.

When Should You Leave the Christian School?

Don and Dottie Williams transferred their three children out of the Christian school and enrolled them in public school. They couldn't get to first base on an educational problem. Dottie, a former educator herself, felt that the teacher, although a lovely Christian person, didn't understand children or teaching methodologies. Furthermore, she refused to discuss the problem or bend. The principal was caught in the middle; he just wanted Dottie to disappear. With only one teacher at her child's grade level, there were few choices.

Deciding to leave the Christian school can often be a traumatic experience for parents. They are torn between their desire for Christian training and the advantages they find in other settings.

Here are six reasons to think about changing schools.

Transfer when the cost becomes prohibitive and you are sacrificing everything for a Christian education
If paying for a Christian education is throwing your budget totally out of whack, perhaps it's time to think of transferring. God doesn't expect you to live in poverty to send your children to school. Eventually, everyone will become resentful. And that's a heavy guilt trip to lay on your kids.

Transfer when the teaching is substandard
While you're probably sending your child to a Christian school for the biblical emphasis, reading the Bible and

praying before each class won't excuse substandard teaching. Your child is in school to learn, and sugarcoating incompetence with spirituality isn't acceptable. If you're paying for the education, you have a right to excellence in teaching.

Transfer when special programs are necessary
Perhaps your child needs special help to catch up. Or maybe your child needs extra enrichment. If your child's educational needs are not being met, think about going where you can get the help you need.

Transfer when the school blames all of your child's problems on your lack of spirituality as a parent
If every parent conference is prefaced with a statement about what is wrong with your child and your family and contains no statements about what the teacher and school are willing to do to help resolve a problem, then it's time to pack up your school bags. Although prayer is powerful and can change things, when the teacher tells you that if you only prayed more, your child would learn his multiplication facts faster, that's stretching it a bit.

Transfer when you have an unresolved conflict with a teacher or administrator
The same advice I gave for public school parents holds true here. If you can't get the problem resolved to everyone's mutual satisfaction, then perhaps a new start in another environment would be beneficial for everyone.

*Transfer when you can no longer support your
school wholeheartedly*
If you are constantly finding fault with every decision,
you're no longer invested in the organization. When
you'd rather complain than pitch in and help, you're not
a team member any longer. Your child has the most
chance of success in a setting that you are supporting
and upholding.

Home Schooling: It's Not for Me

Joylin Lane gets a bit tearful when she talks about her
son attending sixth grade at the Christian school this
year. He's been home-schooled since kindergarten. But
the subject matter is getting more difficult and there are
two younger children who need more of her attention.
Also, the stubbornness and independence of adolescence
are beginning to emerge. Clearly, Matthew is ready for
the change, and so is Mom.

Nancy Probasco has home-schooled her four children
exclusively. The oldest is now in sixth grade. And this
year, for the first time, all but the five-year-old are going
off to public school. Each year she and her husband have
evaluated their situation and vowed that when they
weren't able to give their children what they needed,
they would make the switch. They even went so far as to
"hire" a retired public school teacher to spend some time
each week teaching their children to get them ready for
their new adventure.

There are several good reasons for shutting down your
home school.

Transfer when it's ruining your home life

If the home-schooling issue is a sore point between you and your spouse, it's time to think about a change. You need to be in accord about your child's schooling experience. If your home-schooling has consumed your life to the point that your spouse is no longer important, then you need to re-evaluate your priorities. See if you and your spouse can reach an agreement.

Transfer when you find your own personal development is totally derailed and you have no life of your own

Home schoolers have an intensity and evangelistic zeal that is admirable, if a bit scary at times. A commitment to children that leaves no time for personal interests or future career goals may leave you empty and uninteresting as a person when your children leave the nest.

Transfer when you are not able to make your children do what they are told to do

If your children are suddenly uncooperative and you spend more time talking them into what they have to do than they spend doing it, think about turning them over to someone who is more objective and less involved.

Transfer when your challenging child is running you ragged

If you are the parent of a strong-willed child, you'll need all of the help you can get. While some parents find home schooling to be just the answer for the hyperactive, stubborn child, others don't have the energy or patience to handle it. Even trained teachers need extra help when dealing with strong-willed children. Challenging children need many capable adults in their lives. They wear out people like basketball players wear out shoes.

Transfer when you seem unable to be an effective home schooler

Just because you signed on once doesn't mean you have to do it forever. Sticking with a failing situation just to prove something or save face will be damaging to your children. Have the courage to quit. If you avoid lesson planning, put off making decisions about what to do today indefinitely, and find yourself totally mired down in meaningless detail, put your child in another schooling setting. Recognize when you need help.

Transfer when you and your children are ready for a different learning situation

When your child reaches junior-high or high-school age, he or she may need the challenge of a conventional school setting. Or, a child of any age may be ready for a fresh approach and a new setting. One of the big advantages of being in school is having a variety of teachers, or at least a new one every year. Children will be exposed to teachers who have different personalities, different methodologies, and are experts in a variety of different subjects. Children will gain experience in learning how to get along and please many different kinds of people. You may be getting boring and burned-out if you've been teaching your child for a number of years. Let someone else have a turn.

The most important thing to remember if you're choosing to change is that it's not as traumatic as you think.

Kids are remarkably flexible and adaptable. If they're unhappy, spend time talking with them. Explore the options with them. Let them be a part of the decision. They will feel more ownership of their schooling and their lives, and the educational results will be better.

Schooling Success
for All

---

*M*aybe I'm a little naive to think that all kids can learn. But I don't think so. They just need to be in the right place with the right teacher. Maybe that teacher is Mom and the place is home. For many children, there is no better place. They can mature and develop at their own rate and learn unhindered by the artificial age barriers and stilted structures that often characterize the conventional school settings. Maybe that place is the Christian school where teachers are called of God to teach a curriculum that integrates faith and academics and where like-minded parents and children provide an atmosphere less tainted by the world. Or maybe that place is the public school where values and standards are tested and where the call to be "salt and light" can be practiced.

Fortunately my children have completed their formal education. They are both in college now. I say *fortunately* because writing a book like this can force you to re-examine all of your long-standing beliefs. And what I would want for my children now, since I have gone through the six-step process myself, is for them to have experienced *all* kinds of schools.

Every option has its own unique advantages. The joy that comes from schooling your own children is obvious to see when one talks with home schoolers. These parents are not on the fringes of their children's education; they are intimately involved. The comfort and security that comes from having your children enrolled in a Christian school environment where worries about peer groups and ungodly teachers never cause sleepless nights is enviable. But then there's the pride you feel when you watch your children meet the world on its own turf and never blink, maintaining their faith and advancing it like warriors of old.

Perhaps the best of all worlds is a little of each. But that's for *you* to decide. I won't have to worry about schooling choices again until I have grandchildren.

Notes

Off to School
1. Diane Ravitch. *The Schools We Deserve* (N.Y.: Basic Books, 1985), p. 277.

Chapter 2/The Purpose of Education
1. Mission Statement of Wheaton-Warrenville School District 200, Wheaton, Ill.
2. Claude E. Schindler, Jr. with Pacheco Pyle. *Sowing for Excellence: Educating God's Way* (Whittier, Calif.: Association of Christian Schools International, 1987), pp. 166-167.
3. Bonnie Van Bogelen, "How to Plan and Write Your Own Philosophy of Education," a self-published pamphlet, p. 9.
4. Elaine K. McEwan. *How to Raise a Reader* (Elgin, Ill.: David C. Cook, 1987); *Superkid? Raising Balanced Children in a Superkid World* (David C. Cook, 1988); and *Will My Child Be Ready for School?* (David C. Cook, 1990).

Quotations
John Holt, *Instead of Education: Ways to Help People Do Things Better* (N.Y.: E.P. Dutton & Co., Inc., 1976), pp. 13-14.
William J. Bennett, *First Lessons: A Report on Elementary Education in America* (Washington, D.C.: U.S. Government Printing Office, 1986), p. 3.
National Comission on Excellence in Education, *A Nation at Risk* (Washington, D.C.: U.S. Dept. of Education, 1983), p. 35.
Alan Bloom, *The Closing of the American Mind* (N.Y.: Simon & Schuster, 1987), p. 26.

Chapter 3/What's Best for Your Child?
1. Ralph Matson and Thom Black. *Discovering Your Child's Design* (Elgin, Ill.: David C. Cook Publishing, 1989), pp. 62-65.
2. Ibid., pp. 110-116.
3. Howard Gardner. *Frames of Mind: The Theory of Multiple Intelligences* (N.Y.: Basic Books, 1983).

4. James T. Webb, Elizabeth A. Meckstroth, and Stephanie Nolan. *Guiding the Gifted Child* (Columbus, Ohio: Ohio Psychology Publishing Co., 1982), p. 9.
5. Barbara Meister Vitale. *Unicorns Are Real: A Right Brained Approach to Learning* (Rolling Hills Estate, Calif.: Jalmer Press, 1982), p. 9.
6. Webb, op. cit.
7. Vitale, op. cit.
8. Keith Golay. *Learning Patterns and Temperament Styles* (Fullerton, Calif.: Manas-Systems, 1982), pp. 27-44.
9. Bernice McCarthy and Susan Leflar, eds. *4Mat in Action: Creative Lesson Plans for Teaching to Learning Styles with Right/Left Mode Techniques* (Barrington, Ill.: Excel, 1983).
10. Alexander Thomas and Stella Chess. *Temperament and Development* (New York: Brunner/Mazel Publishers, 1977), pp. 22-23.

Quotations

Keith Golay, *Learning Patterns & Temperament Styles* (Fullerton, Calif.: Manas-Systems, 1982), p. 8.

Ralph Mattson and Thom Black, *Discovering Your Child's Design* (Elgin, Ill.: David C. Cook, 1989), pp. 165-66.

Paul Chance, "Master of Mastery" in *Psychology Today,* April, 1987, p. 46.

Chapter 5/Pros and Cons of Public Schooling

1. Cliff Schimmels. *I Was a High School Drop-In* (N.Y.: Fleming H. Revell, 1986), p. 16.
2. Ibid., p. 156.
3. *Chicago Tribune. Chicago Schools: "Worst in America"* (Chicago, Ill.: The Chicago Tribune, 1988), p. 1.
4. Paul Kienel. *Your Questions Answered about Christian Schools* (Whittier, Calif.: The Association of Christian Schools International, 1983).
5. Tim LaHaye. *The Battle for the Public Schools* (Old Tappan, N.J.: Fleming H. Revell, 1983), p. 13.
6. Schlafly, Phyllis, ed. *Child Abuse in the Classroom* (Alton, Ill.: Pere Marquette Press, 1984), p. 12.
7. Op. cit., p. 13.
8. Nancy Eberle. "Does Home Schooling Pass the Test?" *Woman's Day,* April 14 (1987), p. 32.
9. Melvin Kohn. *Class and Conformity: A Reassessment* (Chicago: University of Chicago Press, 1977).

Quotations

Timothy Jones, Editorial in *Christianity Today,* 22 September, 1989, p. 14.

Nancy Henderson, "Sizing Up Your Local School" in *Changing Times,* November 1989, p. 101.

David Smith in *Schooling Choices: An Examination of Private, Public, & Home Education,* ed. by H. Wayne House (Portland, Oreg: Multnomah, 1988), p. 38.

Jon Barton and John Whitehead, *Schools on Fire: It's Not Too Late to Save the Public Schools* (Wheaton, Ill.: Tyndale House Publishers, Inc., 1980), p. 145.

Stanley M. Elam and Alec M. Gallup, "21st Annual Gallup Poll of the Public's Attitudes Toward the Public Schools" in *Phi Delta Kappan* 71.1, September, 1989.

Sara Lawrence Lightfoot, *Worlds Apart: Relationships Between Families and Schools* (N.Y.: Basic Books, 1978), p. 5.

Charles L. Glenn, "What Evangelicals Should Expect of Public Schools" in *The Reformed Journal,* September, 1986, pp. 12-16.

Cliff Schimmels in *The Blackboard Fumble,* ed. by Ken Sidey (Wheaton, Ill.: Victor Books, 1989), pp. 99-100.

Chapter 6/Christian Schools: God's Mandate for Christians?

1. George Ballweg, "The Growth in the Number and Population of Christian Schools Since 1966: A Profile of Parental Views Concerning Factors Which Led Them to Enroll Their Children in a Christian School" (Ph.D. diss., Boston University School of Education, 1980).

2. H. Wayne House, ed. *Schooling Choices: An Examination of Private, Public & Home Education* (Portland, Oreg.: Multnomah Press, 1988), pp. 110-116.

3. Claude E. Schindler, Jr. with Pacheco Pyle. *Sowing for Excellence: Educating God's Way* (Whittier, Calif.: Association of Christian Schools International, 1987), p. 25.

4. Leslie Tarr, "The Hermetically Sealed World of Neo-Fundamentalism," *Eternity,* August 1976, pp. 24-27.

5. Roy W. Lowrie, Jr. *To Christian School Parents* (Whittier, Calif.: The Association of Christian Schools International, 1982), pp. 105-107.

6. Roy W. Lowrie, Jr. "Marks of a Strong Christian Home," pamphlet published by Christian School Today, 464 Malin Road, Newtown Square, Pennsylvania 1973.

Quotations

Joe Bayly in *The Basis for a Christian School,* ed. by David B. Cummings (Phillipsburg, N.J.: Presbyterian and Reformed Publishing Co., 1982), p. 2.

Alan Peshkin, *God's Choice: The Total World of a Fundamentalist Christian School* (Chicago: University of Chicago Press, 1986), p. 281.

James Coleman, *Public and Private Schools* (Washington, D.C.: National Center for Education Statistics, 1981), p. 43.

Stephen Arons, *Compelling Belief: The Culture of American Schooling* (N.Y.: McGraw-Hill Book Company, 1983), p. 136.

Jeremy Rifkin and Ted Howard, *The Emerging Order: God in an Age of Scarcity* (N.Y.: Ballantine, 1983), p. 128.

Gene I. Maeroff, "Private School Enrollment Takes Off" in *The New York Times,* 3 February, 1985.

Paul A. Kienel, *About Christian School Education* (Whittier, Calif.: Association of Christian Schools International, 1987), pp. 1-4.

Susan Rose, *Keeping Them Out of the Hands of Satan: Evangelical Schooling in America* (N.Y.: Routledge, Chapman and Hall, Inc., 1988), p. 27.

Paul B. Smith, Foreword to *Sowing for Excellence: Educating God's Way*, Claude E. Schindler, Jr. and Pacheco Pyle (Whittier, Calif.: Association of Christian Schools International, 1987), p. iii.

Chapter 7/Home, Sweet Home: Is It the Classroom for You?

1. Nancy Wallace. *Better than School* (N.Y.: Larson, 1983), p. 36.
2. David Elkind. *The Hurried Child: Growing Up Too Fast Too Soon* (Reading, Mass.: Addison-Wesley, 1981).
3. Raymond & Dorothy Moore. *School Can Wait* (Waco, Tex.: Word Books, 1979).
4. David & Micki Colfax. *Home-schooling for Excellence* (Philo, Calif.: Mountain House Press, 1987), p. 95.

Quotations

Gregg Harris in *Schooling Choices: An Examination of Private, Public, & Home Education,* ed. by H. Wayne House (Portland, Oreg: Multnomah, 1988), p. 187.

Raymond and Dorothy Moore, *Home-Grown Kids: A Practical Handbook for Teaching Your Children at Home* (Waco, Tex.: Word Books, 1979), p. 26.

Rousas J. Rushdoony, *Law and Liberty* (Nutley, N.J.: Craig Press, 1971), p. 79.

Brian Ray, "The Kitchen Classroom: Is Home Schooling Making the Grade?" in *Christianity Today,* 12 August, 1988.

Alfie Kohn, "Home-Schooling" in *The Atlantic,* 261:4 (April, 1988), p. 21.

Jean Seligmann with Pamela Abramson in *Newsweek,* 1 February, 1988, p. 49.

David Neff, "Why Johnny Can't Stay Home" in *Christianity Today,* 17 November, 1989.

Stephen Arons, *Compelling Belief: The Culture of American Schooling* (N.Y.: McGraw-Hill Book Company, 1983), pp. 108-109.

Sara Lawrence Lightfoot, *Worlds Apart: Relationships Between Families and Schools* (N.Y.: Basic Books, 1978), p. 187.

Harold G. McCurdy, "The Childhood Pattern of Genius" in *Horizon,* May 1960, pp. 32-38.

Chapter 8/Evaluating Your Options

1. Borg Hendrickson. *Home School: Taking the First Step* (Kooskia, Idaho: Mountain Meadow Press, 1989), p. 261.

Chapter 9/Choosing to Change

Quotations

Sara Lawrence Lightfoot, *Worlds Apart: Relationships Between Families and Schools* (N.Y.: Basic Books, 1978), p. 40.

Bibliography

Armbruster, Frank. *Our Children's Crippled Future: How American Education Has Failed.* N.Y.: Quadrangle/New York Times Book Co., 1977.

Armstrong, Thomas. *In Their Own Way: Discovering and Encouraging Your Child's Personal Learning Style.* Los Angeles: Jeremy P. Tarcher, Inc., 1989.

Arons, Stephen. *Compelling Belief: The Culture of American Schooling.* N.Y.: McGraw-Hill Book Company, 1983.

Ballman, Ray E. *The How and Why of Home Schooling.* Westchester, Ill.: Crossway Books, 1987.

Barton, Jon and John Whitehead. *Schools on Fire: It's Not Too Late to Save the Public Schools.* Wheaton, Ill.: Tyndale House Publishers, Inc., 1980.

Bennett, William J. *First Lessons: A Report on Elementary Education.* Washington D.C.: U.S. Government Printing Office, 1986.

Bloom, Alan. *The Closing of the American Mind.* N.Y.: Simon & Schuster, 1987.

Blumenfeld, Samuel L. *Is Public Education Necessary?* Old Greenwich, Conn.: The Devin-Adair Company, 1981.

Broudy, Harry S. *The Real World of the Public Schools.* N.Y.: Harcourt Brace Jovanovich, Inc., 1972.

Brown, Martha C. *Schoolwise.* Los Angeles: Jeremy P. Tarcher, Inc., 1985.

Chance, Paul. "Master of Mastery." *Psychology Today,* April, 1987.

Chicago Tribune. Chicago Schools: "Worst in America." Chicago: *Chicago Tribune,* 1988.

Coleman, James. *Public and Private Schools*. Washington, D.C.: National Center for Education Statistics, 1981.

Colfax, David and Micki. *Homeschooling for Excellence*. Philo, Calif.: Mountain House Press, 1987.

Cummings, David B., ed. *The Basis for a Christian School*. Phillipsburg, N.J.: Presbyterian and Reformed Publishing Co., 1982.

Cunningham, James D. and Anthony C. Fortosis. *Education in Christian Schools: A Perspective and Training Model*. Whittier, Calif., 1987.

Cutright, Melitta. *The National PTA Talks to Parents: How to Get the Best Education for Your Child*. N.Y.: Doubleday, 1989.

Dunn, Rita and Kenneth Dunn. *Teaching Students through Their Individual Learning Styles*. Reston, Va.: Reston Publishing Co., 1978.

Dyer, Wayne. *What Do You Really Want for Your Children?* N.Y.: Doubleday, 1985.

Eberle, Nancy. "Does Home Schooling Pass the Test?" *Woman's Day,* 14 April, 1989.

Elam, Stanley M. and Alec M. Gallup. "The 21st Annual Gallup Poll of the Public's Attitudes Toward the Public Schools." *Phi Delta Kappan,* 71:1 (September, 1989).

Elkind, David. *The Hurried Child: Growing Up Too Fast Too Soon*. Reading, Mass.: Addison-Wesley, 1981.

Ferguson, Sherry and Lawrence E. Mazin. *Parent Power: A Program to Help Your Child Succeed in School*. N.Y.: Clarkson N. Potter, Inc., Publishers, 1989.

Frith, Terry. *Secrets Parents Should Know About Public School*. N.Y.: Simon & Schuster, 1986.

Gaebelein, Frank. *The Pattern of God's Truth*. Chicago: Moody Press, 1968.

Gardner, Howard. *Frames of Mind: The Theory of Multiple Intelligences*. N.Y.: Basic Books, 1983.

Glenn, Charles L. "What Evangelicals Should Expect of Public Schools." *The Reformed Journal,* September 1986.

Golay, Keith. *Learning Patterns and Temperament Styles*. Fullerton, Calif.: Manas-Systems, 1982, p. 8.

Gorder, Cheryl. *Home Schools: An Alternative*. Tempe, Ariz.: Blue Bird Publications, 1985.

Harris, Gregg. *The Christian Home School*. Brentwood, Tenn.: Wolgemuth & Hyatt, 1987.

Heffley, James C. *Textbooks on Trial*. Wheaton, Ill.: Victor Books, 1976.

Henderson, Nancy. "Sizing Up Your Local School." *Changing Times,* November 1989.

Hendrickson, Borg. *Home School: Taking the First Step*. Kooskia, Idaho: Mountain Meadow Press, 1989.

Holt, John. *Instead of Education: Ways to Help People Do Things Better.* N.Y.: E.P. Dutton & Co., Inc., 1976.

—. *Instead of School: A Hopeful Path for Education*. N.Y.: Dutton, 1976.

—. *Teach Your Own*. New York: Delacorte Press, 1981.

House, H. Wayne, ed. *Schooling Choices:An Examination of Private, Public, & Home Education*. Portland, Oreg.: Multnomah, 1988.

Jones, Timothy. Editorial. *Christianity Today,* 22 September, 1989.

Kienel, Paul A. *About Christian School Education.* Whittier, Calif.: Association of Christian Schools International, 1987.

—. *The Christian School: Why It Is Right for Your Child*. Wheaton, Ill.: Victor Books, 1977.

—. ed. *The Philosophy of Christian School Education*. Whittier, Calif.: Association of Christian Schools International, 1978.

—. *Reasons for Sending Your Child to a Christian School.* LaHabra, Calif.: P.K. Books, 1978.

—. *Your Questions Answered about Christian Schools*. Whittier, Calif.: The Association of Christian Schools International, 1983.

—. *What Every Parent Should Know About Christian School Education.* Whittier, Calif.: Association of Christian Schools International, 1987.

Kohn, Alfie. "Home-Schooling." *The Atlantic,* 261:4 (April, 1988).

LaHaye, Tim. *The Battle for the Public Schools*. Old Tappan, N.J.: Fleming H. Revell, 1983.

Laughy, Linwood. *The Interactive Parent: How to Help Your Child Survive and Succeed in the Public Schools*. Kooskia, Idaho: Mountain Meadow Press, 1988.

Lawrence, Sara Lightfoot (see Lightfoot, Sara Lawrence).

LeFever, Marlene. *Creative Teaching Methods*. Elgin, Ill.: David C. Cook Publishing, 1985.

Lightfoot, Sara Lawrence. *Worlds Apart: Relationships Between Families and Schools*. N.Y.: Basic Books, 1978.

Lines, Patricia M. "An Overview of Home Instruction." *Phi Delta Kappan,* 68:7 (March, 1987).

Lopez, Diane. *Teaching Children: A Curriculum Guide to What Children Need to Know at Each Level through Sixth Grade*. Westchester, Ill.: Crossway Books, 1988.

Lowrie, Roy W., Jr. *Inside the Christian School*. Whittier, Calif.: Association of Christian Schools International, 1980.

—. *To Christian School Parents*. Whittier, Calif.: The Association of Christian Schools International, 1982.

—. *To Those Who Teach in Christian Schools*. Whittier, Calif.: Association of Christian Schools International, 1978.

McCarthy, Bernice and Susan Leflar, eds. *4MAT In Action: Creative Lesson Plans for Teaching to Learning Styles with Right/Left Mode Techniques*. Barrington, Ill.: Excel, 1983.

McCurdy, Harold G. "The Childhood Pattern of Genius." *Horizon*, May 1960.

MacCauley, Susan Schaeffer. *For the Children's Sake*. Westchester, Ill.: Crossway Books, 1984.

McEwan, Elaine K. "Schooling Choices." *Christian Parenting Today*, May/June, 1989.

Maeroff, Gene I. *Don't Blame the Kids*. N.Y.: McGraw-Hill Book Company, 1982.

—. "Private School Enrollment Takes Off." *The New York Times*, 3 February, 1985.

—. *The School-Smart Parent*. N.Y.: Times Books, 1989.

Mattson, Ralph and Thom Black. *Discovering Your Child's Design*. Elgin, Ill.: David C. Cook, 1989.

May, Phillip. *Which Way to Educate?* Chicago: Moody Press, 1975.

Moore, Raymond and Dorothy. *Home-Grown Kids: A Practical Handbook for Teaching Your Children at Home*. Waco, Tex.: Word Books, 1981.

—. *Home-Style Teaching: A Handbook for Parents and Teachers*. Waco, Tex.: Word Books, 1984.

—. *Home-Spun Schools*. Waco, Tex.: Word Books, 1982.

—. *School Can Wait*. Waco, Tex.: Word Books, 1979.

National Commission on Excellence in Education. *A Nation at Risk*. Washington, D.C.: U.S. Dept. of Education, 1983.

Neff, David. "Why Johnny Can't Stay Home." *Christianity Today,* 17 November, 1989.

Nemko, Marty and Barbara Nemko. *How to Get Your Child a "Private School" Education in a Public School*. Washington, D.C.: Acropolis Books, Ltd., 1986.

Pagnoni, Mario. *The Complete Home Educator*. N.Y.: Larson Publications, 1984.

Peshkin, Alan. *God's Choice: The Total World of a Fundamentalist Christian School*. Chicago: University of Chicago Press, 1986.

Pride, Mary. *Big Book of Home Learning*. Westchester, Ill.: Crossway Books, 1986.

—. *The Next Big Book of Home Learning*. Westchester, Ill.: Crossway Books, 1987.

—. *The New Big Book of Home Learning*. Westchester, Ill.: Crossway Books, 1988.

—. *Schoolproof*. Westchester, Ill.: Crossway Books, 1988.

Rafferty, Max. *What They Are Doing to Your Children*. N.Y.: The New American Library of World Literature, Inc., 1963.

Ravitch, Diane. *The Schools We Deserve*. New York: Basic Books, 1985.

Ray, Brian. "The Kitchen Classroom: Is Home Schooling Making the Grade?" *Christianity Today,* 12 August, 1988.

Rich, Dorothy. *Megaskills*. Boston: Houghton Mifflin Company, 1988.

Rifkin, Jeremy and Ted Howard. *The Emerging Order: God in an Age of Scarcity*. N.Y.: Ballantine, 1983.

Rioux, William. *You Can Improve Your Child's School*. N.Y.: Simon and Schuster, 1980.

Rose, Susan. *Keeping Them Out of the Hands of Satan: Evangelical Schooling in America*. N.Y.: Routledge, Chapman and Hall, Inc., 1988.

Rushdoony, Rousas J. *Intellectual Schizophrenia*. Phillipsburg, N.J.: Presbyterian and Reformed Publishing Co., 1980.

—. *Law and Liberty*. Nutley, N.J.: Craig Press, 1971.

Sarason, Seymour B. *Schooling in America: Scapegoat and Salvation*. N.Y.: The Free Press, 1983.

Saunders, Jacqulyn with Pamela Espeland. *Bringing out the Best: A Resource Guide for Parents of Young Gifted Children*. Minneapolis: Free Spirit Publishing Co., 1986.

Schindler, Claude E., Jr. and Pacheco Pyle. *Educating for Eternity*. Wheaton, Ill.: Tyndale House Publishers, Inc., 1979.

—. *Sowing for Excellence: Educating God's Way*. Whittier, Calif.: Association of Christian Schools International, 1987.

Schimmel, David and Louis Fischer. *The Rights of Parents in the Education of Their Children*. Columbia, Md.: National Committee for Citizens in Education, 1977.

Schimmels, Cliff. *How to Shape Your Child's Education*. Elgin, Ill.: David C. Cook Publishing, 1989. Previously published as *How to Help Your Child Thrive and Survive in the Public School*. Old Tappan, N.J.: Fleming H. Revell, 1982.

—. *Notes from the World's Oldest Freshman*. Elgin, Ill.: David C. Cook Publishing, 1989. Previously published as *I Was a High School Drop-In*. Old Tappan, N.J.: Fleming H. Revell, 1986.

—. *Parents' Most-Asked Questions about Kids and Schools.* Wheaton, Ill.: Victor Books, 1989.

Schlafly, Phyllis, ed. *Child Abuse in the Classroom.* Alton, Ill.: Pere Marquette Press, 1984.

Seligmann, Jean with Pamela Abramson. "From Homespun to Harvard." *Newsweek,* 1 February, 1988.

Shackelford, Luanne and Susan White. *A Survivor's Guide to Home Schooling.* Westchester, Ill.: Crossway Books, 1988.

Sidey, Ken, ed. *The Blackboard Fumble.* Wheaton, Ill.: Victor Books, 1989.

Tarr, Leslie K. "The Hermetically Sealed World of Neo-Fundamentalism." *Eternity,* August 1976.

Thomas, Alexander, Stella Chess, and Herbert G. Birch. *Temperament and Development.* N.Y.: Bruner/Mazel Publishers, 1977.

Towns, Elmer L. *Have the Public Schools Had It?* Nashville: Thomas Nelson, 1974.

Vitale, Barbara Meister. *Unicorns Are Real: A Right Brained Approach to Learning.* Rolling Hills Estate, Calif.: Jalmar Press, 1982.

Wade, Theodore E. Jr., et. al. *The Home School Manual.* Auburn, Calif.: Gazelle Publications, 1984.

—. with Dorothy N. Moore and Richard A. Bumstead. *School at Home: How Parents Can Teach Their Own Children.* Colfax, Calif.: Gazelle Publications, 1980.

Wallace, Nancy. *Better Than School.* N.Y.: Larson Publications, 1983.

Webb, James T., Elizabeth Meckstroth, and Stephanie Nolen. *Guiding the Gifted Child.* Columbus, Ohio: Ohio Psychology Publishing Company, 1982.

Whitehead, John and Wendell Bird. *Home Education and Constitutional Liberties.* Westchester, Ill.: Crossway/Good News Publishers, 1984.

Wilson, Stephanie. "Can We Clear the Air About Home Schooling?" *Instructor,* January 1988.

Winkelreid-Dobson, Linda. "I Teach My Kids at Home." *Good Housekeeping,* March 1990.

Wolterstorff, Nicholas. *Educating for Responsible Action.* Grand Rapids: Wm. B. Eerdmans Publishing Company, 1980.

Wynne, Edward. *Looking at Schools: Good, Bad, and Indifferent.* Lexington, Mass.: Lexington Books, 1980.